Hypocrisy or Truth

Do you follow the Church's Hypocrisy, False Traditions & Lies
or do you follow Biblical Truth?

Jesus replied, "And why do you, by your traditions,
violate the direct commandments of God?
Matthew 15:3 (NLT)

Apply Wisdom.com

Hypocrisy or Truth / Paperback -- 1st ed.
ISBN 978-1-946373-00-7
$10.99 everywhere

Hypocrisy or Truth / E-book -- 1st ed.
ISBN 978-1-946373-01-4
Free at ApplyWisdom.com

Table of Contents

Introduction

This book is an attempt to open the eyes of the ones whose hearts are predisposed to see biblical truth and live in accordance with it.

If you have ever tried to go to church but had to leave because you felt that something was off, this book is for you. The church is off basis. It doesn't reflect our loving creator God but reflects the traditions of men.

If you have ever felt an inclination to find and give thanks to (worship) the creator of the universe but were so disgusted by hypocritical Christians that you didn't, this book is for you. Those hypocritical Christians do not speak for the one true God.

This book will be encouraging to those sincerely seeking the truth and seeing the lies of religions. This book will be an emotional reality check for faker and "wannabe" Christians.

Like you, I am sick and tired of false teachings and unbiblical doctrine in the church which make faker, lukewarm Christians out of good and sincere hearted people. I will not water down or sugar coat biblical truths. Expect me to be direct, point out sins and inaccurate thinking, and call "wrong" that which is biblically wrong.

Every single principle discussed in this book I learned the hard way, through pain and tears and regret and research and prayer and forgiveness. It took some "aggressive" discipline from a loving God to open my eyes to my hypocrisy. And so now, in turn, I lovingly write this "aggressive" book to help you open your eyes to see all the lies you have been told, believed and followed.

Because the authority of this book comes from God through His scriptures, if you don't believe that the bible is the inspired word of God then don't bother reading this book. We have no common ground from which to reason. But if you believe in the bible and are dissatisfied with what you see in your church, then please keep reading. You will see what lies your church follows.

If you are agnostic or atheistic, but open to the truth, then please keep reading. I suspect that if you are agnostic or atheistic, it is because you feel an inclination towards a loving creator but are disgusted by the hypocrisy in the modern church. Please keep reading this book as it will help you to realize that the modern catholic and protestant churches do not represent our loving creator God and are more caught up in following the traditions of men at the expense of following the commandments of God.

God doesn't like lukewarm Christians. Revelations 3:15 **I know your deeds, that you are neither cold nor hot. I wish you were cold or else hot. So, because you are lukewarm and neither hot nor cold, I am going to vomit you out of my mouth.**

If you're fed up of with the hypocrisy and lies of religion and the modern church, reading this book and understanding its truth is a step into the right direction because YOU do NOT want to continue being a lukewarm Christian.

A lukewarm Christian reads books written by other lukewarm Christians. A real Christian reads (and studies) the Bible, written under the inspiration of God, by the power of God, which is also known as Holy Spirit. 2 Timothy 3:16-17 **All Scripture is inspired of God and beneficial for teaching, for reproving, for setting things straight, for disciplining in righteousness, so that the man of God may be fully competent, completely equipped for every good work.**

A faker Christian seeks the approval of other silly faker Christians whose eyes are veiled from the truth. A real Christian seeks the approval of our loving Creator who is the author of life.

A hypocrite Christian picks and chooses what he wants to believe and plays with interpretations of the bible. A real Christian is completely obedient to God, not selectively obedient to God.

If you have the courage to read this book, I hope and pray it will give you eyes to see and ears to hear so that you can make the changes needed in your life to become a more authentic and obedient child of the only God.

When we look at the perfect example of Jesus, whose steps we want to follow closely, we see that Jesus was loving to sinners but merciless to the self-righteous religious leaders of his times who missed out on the truth. So in an attempt to follow Jesus closely, I will be as loving as I can. But when we discuss topics which modern day religious leaders ignore or pervert or lie about, please expect me to have an aggressive tone.

This book will discuss dozens of concepts about which the bible is very, very clear. We will mostly discuss simple concepts and principles which everyone should know. I am going to make this book easy to read and easy to understand. It will be incredibly practical. You will read scripture after scripture. I am going to keep my commentary to a minimum. If you have an issue with what this book teaches then please pray about it and read your bible more. Take your issues up with God, since all I am doing is quoting His scriptures.

The inspired Bible reveals a truth which most people seem to ignore: **the unrighteous will not inherit the kingdom of God** (1 Corinthians 6:9). This concept is repeated so many times throughout the bible that it is impossible to dismiss.

Our loving God gave us instructions to follow in order to be righteous. If we are obedient to His commands, we will have peace in this world and everlasting life in God's Kingdom. If we disregard God's standards, we will sadly have to accept the consequences. Ezekiel 16:58 **You will bear the consequences of your obscene conduct and your detestable practices,' declares YHWH.**

If we follow the hypocritical traditions of the church, not biblical truth, we will not be obedient to God. Therefore, it is essential to know the truth. Let us begin....

1. God's Name is YWHW (Yahweh)

Church Hypocrisy / Tradition / Lie: God doesn't have a name but is called "God" or "Lord" or "LORD" or "Jesus."

Biblical Truth: God's name is YHWH and He wants it glorified.

Names are important. Everything has a name. Even your pets have names.

Even every star has a name. Isaiah 40:26 **Raise YOUR eyes high up and see. Who has created these things? It is the One who is bringing forth the army of them even by number, all of whom he calls even by name. Due to the abundance of dynamic energy, he also being vigorous in power, not one [of them] is missing.**

God also has a name. His name is יהוה. These four Hebrew letters are called the Tetragrammaton (which means "four letters") and are most commonly translated as YHWH. Hebrew is read backwards so you can see for yourself that the first and third letters are different and the second and forth letters are the same. All scholars spell the Tetragrammaton YHWH but there is discussion between pronouncing YHWH as Yahweh, Jahweh, or Jehovah. Most languages in the world incorrectly pronounce YHWH as Jehovah while YHWH in Hebrew is pronounced Yahweh.

Yahweh is correct.

Some scholars justify using YHWH by mistakenly mixing the vowels of the Hebrew word *Adonai* (meaning "lord") with YHWH to come up with Y**a**H**o**W**ai**H or Jahovah. This is as historically inaccurate and as ridiculously arbitrary as mixing the vowels of the word *savior* with Jesus and changing God's son's name to J**a**ES**io**US. Obviously this is unreasonable and not academically or historically acceptable. Furthermore, ancient Hebrew did not have vowels. We can't assume the unwritten vowels can be arbitrarily replaced by vowels from a completely different word.

The best and most simple proof of the proper pronunciation of YHWH as Yahweh is the word Halleluiah. When you say or sing this word, which means "praise YHWH," you pronounce the last syllable as "Yah," using a "Y" as in the word "yellow" or "yesterday." The oral tradition of this word has carried on for centuries that the first syllable of YHWH is pronounced as "Yah."

Knowing that our loving heavenly Father has a name is essential. But if you really want to be historically accurate, then say Yahweh.

Many bibles keep the divine name as Yahweh or YHWH. However, the majority of modern bibles change the divine name to LORD (all uppercase letters). More than likely, if you were to read the first few pages of your bible, the translators will explain that they changed YHWH in every occurrence to LORD. The NIV, NLV, ESV, NASV, ISV, and many more translations use LORD.

Unless stipulated otherwise, all referenced scriptures are going to be from the 1984 "New World Translation of the Holy Scriptures" with the exception that I changed back the divine name to the original Hebrew spelling of God's name "YHWH" as it is written in every single original scroll of the Old Testament.

Fact: LORD is simply a title, not a name.

The Merriam-Webster dictionary defines lord as: "one having power and authority over others… a ruler by hereditary right or preeminence to whom service and obedience are due… one of whom a fee or estate is held in feudal tenure… an owner of land or other real property…"

Being called by a title or a description instead of a name is disrespectful and would make someone impatient. Imagine being called by a title rather than your name. To quickly illustrate this point, for the next week call the person you spend the most amount of time with by their title, not their name. See what happens. Let's use my wife as an example. I think she would not like to be called "woman" for the rest of her life. Calling her by her name is more intimate, respectful, and makes a distinction between her and other wives or women. I can hardly imagine calling my children "daughter" or "son" rather than using their first names. After years of praying to YHWH and using the name of YHWH, I could never go back to calling the Creator "LORD" or "God" all the time.

Think about this: A relationship between you and God is very personal and intimate. He is your priority, your God, your friend, and to know and use his name in prayer, and in life, is essential.

Fact: God is a title <u>not</u> a name.

The Merriam-Webster dictionary defines God as: "the supreme or ultimate reality. The being perfect in power, wisdom, and goodness who is worshipped as creator and ruler of the universe. The incorporeal divine Principle ruling over all as eternal Spirit-

Infinite Mind. A being or object believed to have more than natural attributes and powers and to require human worship…"

The bible clearly states that there is only one God, and that his name is YHWH. Psalms 38:18 tells us that YHWH alone is most high: **"That people may know that you, whose name is YHWH, You alone are the Most High over all the earth."**

YHWH is the only God. All else are fake gods and false gods. Isaiah 45: 5-7 **I am YHWH, and there is no one else. With the exception of me there is no God. I shall closely gird you, although you have not known me, in order that people may know from the rising of the sun and from its setting that there is none besides me. I am YHWH, and there is no one else. Forming light and creating darkness, making peace and creating calamity, I, YHWH, am doing all these things.**

Many people falsely assume that the devil took the divine name out of the bible. Of course the devil is glad to hide and obscure the truth about YHWH and his name, but the truth is that YHWH rejected his people (the Jews) and had to separate Himself and His holy name from false worshipers in order to not become defiled and ashamed through association with them.

We will study the Israelites in chapter 37. However, a superficial summary of history reveals that Israel entered into a covenant with YHWH but continually followed the works and examples of the other nations and worshiped foreign (powerless and false) gods. YHWH eventually punished the Israelites so severely that He had to use the Babylonians to conquer Israel and Judah. Yet the Jews did not return to YHWH in heart and mind. Finally, YHWH took His blessing away from them and took His name from them. YHWH now gives his name and blessing to those whose love for Him is pure.

YHWH took his holy name away from the Jews because over and over again, through their disobedience, they profaned it. Jeremiah 44:26 **"Therefore hear the word of YHWH, all you of Judah who are living in the land of Egypt: "Here I swear by my own great name," says YHWH, "that my name will no longer be called on in an oath by any man of Judah in all the land of Egypt who says, 'As surely as the Sovereign Lord YHWH is alive!**

YHWH had to take away his name from the Jews to keep it sacred. (Ezekiel 36:21-23) **I will show concern for my holy name, which the house of Israel profaned among the nations where they have gone." "Therefore say to the house of Israel, this is what the Sovereign Lord YHWH says: "Not for your sakes am I acting, O house of Israel, but for my holy name, which you profaned among the nations**

where you have gone." 'I will certainly sanctify my great name, which was profaned among the nations, which you profaned among them; and the nations will have to know that I am YHWH,' declares the Sovereign Lord YHWH, 'when I am sanctified among you before their eyes.

The Jews developed a superstition that it was bad or dangerous to say YHWH. Amos prophesied about the near future when Israelites would develop a superstition about using the name of YHWH. (Amos 6:10) **A relative will come to carry them out and burn them one by one. He will bring their bones out from the house; then he will say to whoever is in the inner rooms of the house, 'Are there any more with you?' And he will say, 'Nobody!' Then he will say, 'Keep silent! For it is not the time to make any mention of the name of YHWH.'**

The devil has taken advantage of YHWH's desire to only associate His name with those who honor Him. The devil loves to hide the name of YHWH, diminish YHWH's influence, and divert love for YHWH by grouping YHWH together with so many other false gods. The great deceiver (the devil) has successfully made people think there are many gods out there and that the god of the bible is just one of them.

Original text and manuscripts of the bible write YWHW around 7000 times. Yet, to misdirect the prestige and honor of YHWH or to sell more bibles, many translations have written out the divine name.

If you were a part of a bible translation project which agreed to write out the name YHWH and maliciously replace it with LORD, woe to you. You remind me of the words of Jesus in John 8:44 **YOU are from YOUR father the Devil, and YOU wish to do the desires of YOUR father. That one was a manslayer when he began, and he did not stand fast in the truth, because truth is not in him. When he speaks the lie, he speaks according to his own disposition, because he is a liar and the father of [the lie].**

Shame on you if you are a leader in the church and don't teach your flock about the divine name or understand that the bible translation you use diminishes the honor due to YHWH.

It is very important to know and glorify the name of God. Jesus states in one of the most memorized scriptures of all times the importance of the divine name. Matthew 6:9-10 (KJV) **Our Father which art in heaven, Hallowed be thy name. Thy kingdom come. Thy will be done in earth, as it is in heaven.**

It is impossible to glorify the name of God if you don't know it. Just think how ironic the above scripture is because of the millions and millions of faker Christians who daily or weekly say **"hallowed be thy name"** (King James Version) and yet don't even know that His name is YHWH. Jesus said in the model prayer that His Father's name (YHWH) must be glorified.

If you did not know that our Heavenly Father has a name, then congratulations on learning one of the first and most important facts of life. Your church leadership should have shown you this important fact years ago.

YHWH wants his name to be gloried and it will be glorified. YHWH even says it himself in Ezekiel 39:7 **And my holy name I shall make known in the midst of my people Israel, and I shall no more let my holy name be profaned; and the nations will have to know that I am YHWH, the Holy One in Israel.** Psalm 86:9 tells us that "**all the nations whom you have made will themselves come, and they will bow down before you, O YHWH, and will give glory to your name.**" Psalms 34:3 reads: **"O magnify YHWH with me, YOU people, and let us exalt his name together."**

Don't misuse the name of the YHWH. Exodus 20:7 **You must not take up the name of YHWH your God in a worthless way, for YHWH will not leave the one unpunished who takes up his name in a worthless way**.

Most faker Christians don't know that the 10 commandments are listed in two places in the bible: Exodus 20 and Deuteronomy 5. Most think that interpreting this commandment about misusing YHWH's name means we should never say things like "oh my god," or in a moment of anger say "Jesus Christ!" Sure, this is bad, and depending on the exact phrase, absolutely disrespectful. But the greater sin is when you profess to be a Christian but live a hypocritical and sinful life identical to the atheist next door. That is how you truly blaspheme the name of YHWH.

Approximately 7000 times in our scriptures YHWH is used. There is only one true God and YHWH is his name. And this is a truth that every single human being who has ever lived will come to know (the hard way or the easy way). My prayer and hope is that you will accept this truth now and work to glorify the name of YHWH from now on.

2. Obedience is Essential

Church Hypocrisy / Tradition / Lie: Take and Leave some parts of the Bible. Do what you want.

Biblical Truth: Obedience is Essential. YHWH's rules are designed to give you peace and joy and abundant, everlasting life.

Hypocrites follow traditions of men not the bible. Matthew 15:3 **In reply he said to them: "Why is it YOU also overstep the commandment of God because of YOUR tradition?"**

Real Christians pay attention and are obedient. Isaiah 48: 17-18 **This is what YHWH has said, your Repurchaser, the Holy One of Israel: "I, YHWH, am your God, the One teaching you to benefit [yourself], the One causing you to tread in the way in which you should walk. O if only you would actually pay attention to my commandments! Then your peace would become just like a river, and your righteousness like the waves of the sea.**

Only a few are chosen. Matthew 7: 21-23 **Not everyone saying to me, 'Lord, Lord,' will enter into the kingdom of the heavens, but the one doing the will of my Father who is in the heavens will. Many will say to me in that day, 'Lord, Lord, did we not prophesy in your name, and expel demons in your name, and perform many powerful works in your name?' And yet then I will confess to them: I never knew YOU! Get away from me, YOU workers of lawlessness.**

This is an essential scripture for understanding obedience. We see that Jesus, the fair judge, will say he never knew people in verse 22 who call Jesus "**Lord, Lord**" and who did amazing works in his name. Back in the time of Jesus, to say someone's name twice was to imply intimacy with them. This means they loved Jesus. To call Jesus LORD (all capital letters) would mean that they confused him (Jesus) with YHWH. So to call him Lord (Only the L in capital letters) means their doctrine was correct and they knew Jesus to be their master, leader, and the son of God. And wow, these people did great works like prophecy and expel demons. Yet Jesus never knew them. Simply loving Jesus is not enough. And having correct doctrine is not enough. And doing great works is not enough. Obedience to YHWH is perhaps what makes the difference.

If you have a lack of common sense or judgment and believe the twisted Calvinistic teaching of "once saved, always saved," then please reread Matthew 7:13-23 (above) and pray about Philippians 2:12: **Consequently, my beloved ones, in the way that YOU have always obeyed, not during my presence only, but now much more**

readily during my absence, keep working out YOUR own salvation with fear and trembling.

Fear God and be Obedient. Ecclesiastes 12:13 **The conclusion of the matter, everything having been heard, is: Fear the [true] God and keep his commandments. For this is the whole [obligation] of man.**

Be a slave of Obedience. Romans 6:16 **Do YOU not know that if YOU keep presenting yourselves to anyone as slaves to obey him, YOU are slaves of him because YOU obey him, either of sin with death in view or of obedience with righteousness in view?**

The current world situation is a consequence of disobedience. Deuteronomy 28:19 **Cursed will you be when you come in, and cursed will you be when you go out.**

It is too easy to drift away from biblical teachings. If you follow the people on your left and right at church then you will quickly drift. If you follow your spiritual leaders you will quickly drift. If you follow the leaders of the world, the movie and music stars, the sports heroes, the "role models," or the lifestyle trends of this world then you are going to drift.

Friendship with the world means being an enemy of God. James 4:4 **Adulteresses, do YOU not know that the friendship with the world is enmity with God? Whoever, therefore, wants to be a friend of the world constitutes himself an enemy of God.**

Love for YHWH means obedience. 1 John 5:3-**For this is what the love of God means, that we observe his commandments; and yet his commandments are not burdensome.**

I can't stress obedience enough. The bible is so clear on this point. You must be obedient to what YHWH says through the scriptures. You can't be a Christian and in a right standing with YHWH if you are disobedient. The rest of the book will focus on ways most people have been led astray from obedience and from the truth. But first, let's make a quick summary of the one who loves to deceive and lead people away from YHWH.

3. Satan is Real

Church Hypocrisy / Tradition / Lie: Satan is figurative. The world is basically good.

Biblical Truth: Satan is real and he hates you and wants to kill you using direct or indirect methods.

In a book about how to better love and obey YHWH, I do not want to spend too much time on Satan. But he and his workers exists and so we must address them.

Consider this illustration: YHWH is a loving teacher in the math class of life and Satan is a bad student. YHWH is teaching long division to myriads and **myriads of angels** (Revelation 5:11) and to billions of humans. Satan stands up and defiantly tells everyone that YHWH is a liar and that he (Satan) has a better way of doing the long division of life. YHWH could have crushed Satan for his disobedience and disrespect. But if YHWH would have crushed Satan then the rest of the angels could have eventually developed doubt and though that YHWH crushed Satan because Satan was right. This doubt could have eventually caused other angels to rebel. Thankfully, YHWH invites Satan to the chalk board and allows Satan to prove before the entire class that his way for doing the long division of life doesn't lead to the solution. By doing this, all the angels in the classroom see that YHWH's ways are best and that Satan is the liar. We are now in the final days of Satan's system of things. Satan has proven that his ways of life do not feed the poor, maintain justice, inspire love, and give peace. Satan's way of doing the long division of life is in the final days of proving itself wrong.

We are warned in Ephesians that our struggle is against wicked spirit forces. Ephesians 6:11-12 **Put on the complete suit of armor from God that YOU may be able to stand firm against the [methods] of the Devil; because we have a wrestling, not against blood and flesh, but against the governments, against the authorities, against the world rulers of this darkness, against the wicked spirit forces in the heavenly places.**

Satan is a man killer and the father of the lie. We see this truth when Jesus is righteously shredding to pieces the hypocritical religious leaders of his time. John 8:44 **YOU are from YOUR father the Devil, and YOU wish to do the desires of YOUR father. That one was a manslayer when he began, and he did not stand fast in the truth, because truth is not in him. When he speaks the lie, he speaks according to his own disposition, because he is a liar and the father of [the lie].**

Satan's origins are from long ago when he was a fallen angel. Isaiah 14: 12-15 **"O how you have fallen from heaven, you shining one ("Lucifer" in KJV), son of**

the dawn! How you have been cut down to the earth; you who were disabling the nations! As for you, you have said in your heart, 'To the heavens I shall go up. Above the stars of God I shall lift up my throne, and I shall sit down upon the mountain of meeting, in the remotest parts of the north. I shall go up above the high places of the clouds; I shall make myself resemble the Most High.' "However, down to Sheol you will be brought, to the remotest parts of the pit.

Satan has many followers (also fallen angels who ignored their assigned role in heaven) and we usually call them demons. In Genesis 6:1-5 we read about angels who came down to earth right before the time of the flood to take wives from the daughter of men. Jesus in several places in the gospels cast out demons (Matthew 8:16, Matthew 12:22, Matthew 17:18.).

When the hypocritical religious leaders of Jesus' time were slandering Jesus, they said he (Jesus) was using the power of Satan, the "ruler of demons". Matthew 12: 24 **At hearing this, the Pharisees said: "This fellow does not expel the demons except by means of Beelzebub, the ruler of the demons."**

The deceiver is described as the one misleading the entire earth. Revelations 12:9 **So down the great dragon was hurled, the original serpent, the one called Devil and Satan, who is misleading the entire inhabited earth; he was hurled down to the earth, and his angels were hurled down with him.**

This world is lying in the power of the evil one. 1 John5:19 **We know we originate with God, but the whole world is lying in the [power of the] wicked one.** This truth is one which many do not want to accept. Of course, YHWH is in charge and sovereign and all capable. But Satan runs the world right now. It only takes a minute to see that human governments have failed man, and that starvation, death, sin, and selfishness abound. Is that a reflection of our holy God of love? No way. The only answer to the problems of this world is God's Kingdom, which will set it all straight again. That is why Jesus said in Matthew 9: 9-10 **"YOU must pray, then, this way: 'Our Father in the heavens, let <u>your name</u> be sanctified. Let <u>your kingdom</u> come. Let <u>your will</u> take place, as in heaven, also upon earth."** Nothing short of YHWH's kingdom coming will end the evil effects of Satan upon the current system of things.

Satan's first sentence referenced in the bible ignored the name of YHWH, used the word "God," and was a distracting lie designed to turn Eve and Adam away from YHWH. Genesis 3:1 **"now the serpent proved to be the most cautious of all the wild beasts of the field that YHWH God had made. So it began to say to the woman: "Is it really so that God said: YOU must not eat from every tree of the garden?"** First of all, Satan knows the name of YHWH and did not use it. What a deceiver. Secondly, by using the word god, he begins the process of implying that there can be other gods out there who have power. As it turns out, thousands of years later, Satan has been successful in accomplishing this and the world now thinks there are thousands of other gods out there. But the truth is, there is only one god, and His name is YHWH. Thirdly, Satan twists the words of YHWH to infuse doubt and question YHWH's sovereignty.

We see from Genesis 2:16-17 that YHWH said eat from all the trees, just not the tree of knowledge: "**And YHWH God also laid this command upon the man: "From every tree of the garden you may eat to satisfaction. But as for the tree of the knowledge of good and bad you must not eat from it, for in the day you eat from it you will positively die.**" Yet Satan twists words to make YHWH seem unreasonable. From the first sentence out of his mouth, Satan is deceiving and misdirecting and trying to make people wonder off from YHWH.

The deceiver hates YHWH and wants to steal kill and destroy. John 10:10 **The thief does not come unless it is to steal and slay and destroy. I have come that they might have life and might have it in abundance.** But when the deceiver is finally defeated and **"hurled into the lake of fire and sulphur"** (Revelations 20:10), no one will ever have even know his name.

"Satan" is not a name but a descriptive name. It means "resister". The "devil" is not a name but a descriptive name. It means "slanderer." "Beelzebub," or "Baalzebub," is a Philistine god and is commonly translated "the lord of the flies".[1] As we discussed a few paragraphs ago, "Lucifer" is a name given by only the King James version to the "shining one," and is a symbolic reference to Satan but a literal prophecy (which came true) against Babylon.

We are encouraged to not be ignorant of Satan's methods. 2 Corinthians 2: 11 **that we may not be overreached by Satan, for we are not ignorant of his designs.**

Satan uses as many methods for pulling people away from worshiping YHWH as he can. In the bible, we read many stories about Satan hurting people through demon possession. That doesn't happen much these days. Satan has it easier these days to mislead people because sin is everywhere. Let us just take two simple examples: Pornography and Materialism. Not long ago, to obtain pornography, people had to go to a sex shop. Today, people are just a click away from pornographic material via the internet. Not long ago, to purchase something expensive you had to save for a long time then pay it in cash or in trade. Today, the world tells you: "buy today and

---

[1] New Advent, Catholic Encyclopedia, http://www.newadvent.org/cathen/02388c.htm

pay tomorrow." Credits and credit cards are the most used payment methods in this materialistic world and I do not need to tell you that materialism is a dangerous trap.

Satan and his demons are very successful when they transform themselves into false angels and ministers. 2 Corinthians 11: 14-15 **And no wonder, for Satan himself keeps transforming himself into an angel of light. It is therefore nothing great if his ministers also keep transforming themselves into ministers of righteousness. But their end shall be according to their works.** This is an essential scripture for understanding the lies that your church has been telling you throughout your entire life.

This book is an attempt to open the eyes of the ones whose hearts are predisposed to see the truth and live in accordance with it.

The reason so many don't see the truth is that they follow the lies and false teachings of their ministers who are following demons pretending to be angels of light or ministers of righteousness. We will address the policies and effects of Satan pretending to be a religious leaders or a (false) god in future chapters of this book.

Satan has bombarded the world with many false religions, which tell people what they want to hear. 2 Timothy 4:3-4 **For there will be a period of time when they will not put up with the healthful teaching, but, in accord with their own desires, they will accumulate teachers for themselves to have their ears tickled; and they will turn their ears away from the truth, whereas they will be turned aside to false stories.**

To conclude this chapter I want to do a quick simplification of life. On the good side you have YHWH and his angels. Period. On the bad side you have the devil and his followers who are demons. YHWH gave us directions for life and truth as known through the scriptures. Satan is misleading the entire world to pull people away from pure worship of YHWH. There are only two sides. That is why Jesus said in Matthew 12:30 **"He that is not on my side is against me, and he that does not gather with me scatters."** There is only one God and his name is YHWH.

All false gods are nothing other than demons leading many people astray. Let's take just three examples: Buddha, Allah, and the Mormon god. Buddha's real name was Siddhartha Gotama, a man born in 563 BC who spent all 80 years of his life in a place now called Nepal. He was not, nor did he claim to be a god. He was a man who taught a path to enlightenment from his own experience. Satan has exploited this enlightenment and now billions have been led away from the only, true, living God.

Another man, named Mohamed, was manipulated by Satan to write down false prophecies and make declarations about another false and powerless god, Allah. Of course, Mohamed existed and actually heard a miraculous voice. But the truth is that what he heard was not from the true God, YHWH, but was a demon pretending to be the false god, Allah. It is interesting to note that Allah is not a name but is just a title. When translated, Allah means nothing else but "Lord" or "Master." Billions of Muslims have been misled into following a powerless and nameless "master."

The false god of the Mormon church is the same. A demon, pretending to be god, manipulated Joseph Smith to create another false religion. As a result, millions of nice people have been misled away from the truth.

Modern day faker Christians who "hear from god" or "hear from Jesus" are nothing more than men and women who are being manipulated by demons.

The tactic of pretending to be a false god to mislead people from YHWH is nothing new for Satan. He has always been a deceiver. In the upcoming chapters, let's look at several ways in which Satan has misled the modern church, and many of you, to believe many things not in the bible.

4. Men Need to Grow Up

Church Hypocrisy / Tradition / Lie: Mediocrity and apathy are OK.

Biblical Truth: The sinfulness of men is the cause of so much, absolutely avoidable, pain.

All men are sinners and fall short of the glory of God. Romans 3:23 **For all have sinned and fall short of the glory of God**.

Despite all men being sinners, some men do their best to honor YHWH with every aspect of their lives. These men are the rare exceptions, because the overwhelming majority of men on this planet are silly, selfish, knuckle-headed boys who continue to hurt loved ones and make this world more evil.

The point of this chapter is to illustrate that men and their sinfulness is the cause of so many of our problems. Although women are not perfect either, they are mostly the victims. Men and their sinfulness have caused billions to suffer. Let's look at three major examples of their sinfulness: lack of leadership, sexual sin, and financial sin.

<u>Lack of male leadership</u> has destroyed the family: YHWH designed the family before He designed the church and worship. YHWH designed man to be the head of the household and to be the leader of the family.

Man is the head of the family. 1 Corinthians 11:3 **But I want YOU to know that the head of every man is the Christ; in turn the head of a woman is the man; in turn the head of the Christ is God.**

YHWH holds men responsible for their role as leaders. Sadly, men have become lethargic and have let women usurp their God given leadership role. This makes a disharmony in the family, a reverse leadership disharmony. For example, I have noticed that most of the time when we are watching a documentary on TV, the wife does all the talking and the man stands there like a silly child. Most of the households I know are run by the wives. Rather than providing Godly leadership under which the wife is free to flourish, the men let the wives lead, the men let the wives work, and the men let the wives provide.

YHWH wants and requires men to provide. 1 Timothy 5:8 **Certainly if anyone does not provide for those who are his own, and especially for those who are members of his household, he has disowned the faith and is worse than a person without faith.** What this means is that all the dead beat husbands out there who do not work to provide for their families or who make their wives work to provide for the families are worse than unbelievers. YHWH places great importance upon accepting your role in life and the woman's role is not to be the provider.

Sadly, this "weak husband" dysfunction is so normal that men who act like boys has become the standard, not the exception. As a result of sinful men and their pathetic leadership, the biblical family rarely exists.

Men let women do the talking, leading, teaching. Women are now leaders at home, in the work force, in politics, and in the faker church. All of this has consequences:

1. Wives have to work outside the home: This is not part of YHWH's plan. Women were designed to be helpmates, run the household, and raise wonderful children. YHWH's design for a woman is to be a worker at home. Titus 2:3-**5 Likewise let the aged women be reverent in behavior, not slanderous, neither enslaved to a lot of wine, teachers of what is good; that they may recall the young women to their senses to love their husbands, to love their children, to be sound in mind, chaste, workers at home, good, subjecting themselves to their own husbands, so that the word of God may not be spoken of abusively.** If a wife works for materialistic reasons and to buy more luxuries, then this is not biblical. Material reasons overtake legitimate needs. Of course if the family situation is drastic, and the wife needs to help her husband to provide for the family, there is nothing to say. But don't forget the bible says that the man is clearly the provider (1 Timothy 5:8).

2. Kids are raised by strangers: Kids no longer grow up with a stay at home mother who teaches them biblical values and principles. Kids are raised by strangers who don't have the same values.

3. Families drift away from YHWH: 99% of families where the mother works are families that worship money more than YHWH. A family that sends kids to day care so they can earn more money worships money more than YHWH. Day care employees are not going to teach your kids about YHWH. The bible says not to be unequally yoked with non-believers.

A man who lets his kids be raised by strangers or by an unspiritual wife neglects the commandments of YHWH and is yoked together with unbelievers. 2 Corinthians 6:14 **Do not become unevenly yoked with unbelievers. For what fellowship do righteousness and lawlessness have.**

Men, if you don't love your fragile wives well you will not have the approval of YHWH and He will not listen to your prayers. 1 Peter 3: 7 **YOU husbands, continue**

dwelling in like manner with them according to knowledge, assigning them honor as to a weaker vessel, the feminine one, since YOU are also heirs with them of the undeserved favor of life, in order for YOUR prayers not to be hindered. This scripture is great because it reminds all of us that YHWH's love is undeserved (grace). Yet it further reminds men that in order to have their prayers heard they need to treat their wives well.

Evil men and their Sexual sin cause so much pain. Sexual sin destroys the family, destroys women, and destroys peoples' sense of right and wrong.

1. Evil men and their sexual sin destroy the family. Statistics about divorce get worse and worse every year. Stupid and disloyal men seek pleasure through an immoral affair. Evil men who love themselves more than YHWH or their spouse or children want to "upgrade" their wives for a younger woman and in doing so kill the spirit of their wives and family. Single mothers now have to get a job to pay the bills since their idiot husbands no longer provide for them. Rather than serving, loving, and raising children the single mother must work for the rest of her life to survive.

2. Evil men and their sexual sin destroy women: When a selfish man treats a woman terribly it leaves a life-long scar. Men and their evil lusts for skinnier, younger woman has caused millions of women to hurt themselves and be completely unnatural in their efforts to be skinnier and look younger.

3. Evil men and their sexual sin destroy peoples' sense of right and wrong. Because men are evil, sex sells. Men love to look at sinfulness which has caused women to do unladylike things and wear unladylike clothes to get men's attention. Sex is now a part of every advertisement, movie, magazine and commercial. Most people have become so familiar with this sinful sexuality that they don't even notice that their TV commercial is as perverted as pornography.

Jesus reminds us that we are not even to keep on looking at a woman who is not your wife. Matthew 5:27-28 **"You heard that it was said: 'You must not commit adultery.' But I say to you that everyone who keeps on looking at a woman so as to have a passion for her has already committed adultery with her in his heart.** Sadly, Satan has succeeded at making men sexually perverted and adulterers.

Financial Sin has destroyed the world. Because sinful men love things and use people, rather than love people and use things, they spend all their lives worshiping money.

You can't serve two masters. Matthew 6:24 **"No one can slave for two masters; for either he will hate the one and love the other, or he will stick to the one and despise the other. YOUcannot slave for God and for Riches.**

Because men worship money not YHWH they have drifted away from YHWH, destroyed the family, ruined the earth.

1. Worshiping money makes silly men drift away from YHWH: Because sinful men love themselves and want to be happy, they spend their time pursuing and worshiping things, possessions, and temporary happiness, rather than YHWH the author of life and source of eternal happiness.

2. Worshiping money destroys the family: Because men are selfish, they believe the family should make them happy. Rather than investing in the family, they suck the life and joy out of their family. And when they realize that they are not happy, they leave their family in pursuit of freedom or of another family, which they think will make them happy. This sinful mindset destroys the biblical institution of the family and leaves so many devastated children and women in its wake.

3. Worshiping money ruins the earth: If someone loves YHWH with their all and loves their neighbor as themselves then they are not going to pollute the earth. Factories, power plants, ozone destroyers, vehicle smog, oil spills and so on are because men want to be rich more than they want to enjoy the earth forever. Global warming is nothing more than a symptom of man worshiping his real god, money.

A real man does all things for YHWH's glory. Corinthians 10:31 **Do all things for God's glory.**

An evil man does what he can to make himself happy and seek his own temporary benefit, even at the cost of destroying the family, his loved ones, his kids, his wife, and the earth.

If only all men would be obedient to what the scriptures command and try to honor YHWH with everything they do.

5. Entertainment must be Wholesome

Church Hypocrisy / Tradition / Lie: Do what everyone else in the world does, but go to church on Sunday.

Biblical Truth: Honor YHWH with your recreation.

True Christians don't do, read, watch, or enjoy stupid (bad) things. True Christians do not participate in anything unwholesome, unclean, sexually immoral, violent...etc.

A Christian must train his conscience so that he will not feast on the entertainment this world has to offer.

Do all things for YHWH's glory. Corinthians 10:31 **Do all things for God's glory**

YHWH loves us and wants us to be happy. He gave us biblical principles to live by so that we can actually have happiness and joy. YHWH gave us a Sabbath so we can rest. He gave us wonderful food to enjoy. He created us with a desire to have fellowship and be social. He gave us a desire to have recreation and entertainment and music and laughter and joy. But Satan has perverted the world so much that most people wittingly and unwittingly partake of unwholesome and evil entertainment. Please reassess what you do for entertainment and how you do it, making sure that they are in accordance with biblical principles, not in accordance with what everyone else in the world does.

Let's look at some guideline scriptures and principles about the ways of the world (to include entertainment) and the ways of a true Christian. In summary: The world is evil. The devil wants to steal, kill and destroy. True Christians want to stay holy. True Christians want to honor God, even at the expense of not being cool. True Christians don't read, watch, and enjoy stupid things.

The world is evil. 1 John 5:19 We know we originate with God, but the whole world is lying in the [power of the] wicked one.

The devil wants to steal, kill, destroy. John 10:10 The thief does not come unless it is to steal and slay and destroy. I have come that they might have life and might have it in abundance.

The devil is always looking to pounce on you. 1Peter 5:8 Keep YOUR senses, be watchful. **YOUR** adversary, the Devil, walks about like a roaring lion, seeking to devour [someone].

True Christians want to stay holy.

Don't defile your eyes. Job 31:1 **"A covenant I have concluded with my eyes. So how could I show myself attentive to a virgin?**

Lust begins with the eyes. Matthew 5:28 But I say to **YOU** that everyone that keeps on looking at a woman so as to have a passion for her has already committed adultery with her in his heart.

Don't look at worthless things. Psalm 119:37 **Make my eyes pass on from seeing what is worthless; Preserve me alive in your own way.**

True Christians want to honor God, even at the expense of not being "cool" or "in." True Christians want to honor God by rejecting all kind of unwholesome entertainment, abhorring what is wicked and consistently turning away from what is bad.

The goal of this chapter is to help you develop faith without hypocrisy. 1 Tim.1:5 **the objective of this instruction is love out of a clean heart and out of a good conscience and out of faith without hypocrisy.**

Friendship with the world is wrong. James 4:4 Adulteresses, do **YOU** not know that the friendship with the world is enmity with God? Whoever, therefore, wants to be a friend of the world is constituting himself an enemy of God.

Please listen to this counsel so you don't drift away from God. Hebrews 2:1 That is why it is necessary for us to pay more than the usual attention to the things heard by us, that we may never drift away.

Guard your heart by not looking at evil things. Proverbs 4:23 More than all else that is to be guarded, safeguard your heart, for out of it are the sources of life. The more you look at immoral things the quicker your heart turns evil. The more you look at violent movies and video games the quicker your heart becomes hard, loveless. YHWH wants us to be pure of heart.

It is so easy to sin with your eyes. John 9:41 Jesus said to them: "If **YOU** were blind, **YOU** would have no sin. But now **YOU** say, 'We see.' **YOUR** sin remains."

Let's look at several common examples of where fakers Christians disregard biblical principles every day in their quest to be entertained:

<u>Movies:</u> The entertainment of this world is mostly ugly and defiled and has led so many people off the path of biblical cleanliness. Wake Up. If you watch R rated (R=Restricted for adults only) movies then you are a faker Christian. Shame on you. The sex and violence of R rated movies burns your consciousness and rips you away from your Holy Father. If you watch PG-13 (Parental Guidance required for people

under 13 years old) movies then you are a faker Christian. Shame on you, too. Do you think that 50% less violence or sex or inappropriate innuendos make it OK for you to watch? Your conscious is already burned and you are already ripped away from your Holy Father in heaven.

PG and G (Parental Guidance and General) rated movies are just as bad and once you have a YHWH trained conscious, you will have a hard time watching any movies or TV shows available through Satan's film and TV industry.

What you probably don't see because your eyes are not open is that a constantly increasing number of kid's movies teach you that witchcraft and spiritualism is cool. These practices are strictly forbidden in the scriptures. Friendly ghosts and vampires and materialism and gossip and homosexuality have become cool.

Scary movies no longer scare people because their hearts are so calloused. Most of the Romance movies now a day contain fornication (premarital or extramarital sex) which the scriptures forbid and you think it was a sweet and romantic movie.

How many times are you going to slap YHWH in the face with the decisions you make concerning entertainment?

YHWH tells us to guard our hearts. (Proverbs 4:23) **More than all else that is to be guarded, safeguard your heart, for out of it are the sources of life.** Your heart has two main vulnerabilities: your eyes and ears. Watching stupid movies destroys these two layers and ruins your heart. YHWH judges the heart. What does that tell you about where you stand with Him?

Not all movies are bad. Many movies are wonderfully fun or educational or entertaining. A true Christian has to be very deliberate about guarding their heart and eyes and conscious when watching movies.

Almost all major <u>magazines</u> out there are trash. Let me clarify: in America, many are evil, most are trash. They are full of gossip, sex, lies, materialism. The women and men who pose half naked on the covers of your magazines are no better than prostitutes. They will wear anything or endorse anything for money. Fashion magazines sold to millions of women each month are an amazingly effective tool of the devil to cause lust of the eyes, physical insecurity, pervert YHWH's plan for marriage and sexuality, smash consciousness, and ruin marriages. Trashy tabloids and gossip and humanistic feel good magazines encourage you to love the world more than God and steer you off course. Guard your conscious by not wasting your time with that trash.

Books: True Christians don't read unwise things. What we read is just as important as what we see. Don't think for a second that a 300 page book which has sold millions of copies is any less an instrument of Satan than a trashy magazine. Reading a trashy book which pulls you away from the living God is not good. Wasting our precious time reading things which glamorize materialism and the rich and famous (who are 100% all faker Christians or not Christians at all) is not good. Honoring God with what we see and read is good.

Junk **in** will mean junk **out**. But good **in** can mean good **out**.

Television is an amazing source of filth and evil. Faker Christians love to watch Satan's television. Even if you are watching something good and clean it won't surprise anyone if the first commercial is for condoms, beer, herpes medicine, a sexually explicit soap opera, or a shampoo brand demonstrating their product with half naked models. How sad it is that men are so sinful and so easily distracted by skin. The effects of men and their sexual sin is evident the second you turn on the television. Satan wants to place before you anything he can to pull you away from YHWH. A real Christian has to be very deliberate about guarding their heart and eyes and conscious when watching TV.

Consider the internet a reflection of your heart. If you have a pure heart, you use it for shopping, learning, research, coordinating directions, weather, e-mail. If you have no conscious, then you look at evil things. If you have no peace in life and are empty inside, you use the internet for distraction by using your social networking site every hour, playing video games, checking your e-mail 10 times a day, and catching up on gossip. If your existence is more exciting online than in reality you have a sad life and really need make changes so as to live it in accordance with biblical principles.

Pornography is another very popular form of entertainment, one which comes directly from Satan himself. Many faker Christian leaders love porn. When you look at the statistics about porn there is no difference between the number of atheists who look at porn and the number of ministers or regular church attenders who also look at porn. "63% of pastors surveyed confirm that they are struggling with sexual addiction or sexual compulsion including, but not limited to, the use of pornography, compulsive masturbation, or other secret sexual activity."[2] What a shame.

- Men are 543% *more* likely to look at porn than females.
- Those who are happily married are 61% *less* likely to look at porn.

[2] http://www.expastors.com/how-many-pastors-are-addicted-to-porn-the-stats-are-surprising/

- Regular church attenders are 26% *less* likely to look at porn than non-attenders, but those self-identified as "fundamentalists" are 91% *more* likely to look at porn.[3]

What a slap in God's face. The Bible challenges us in Proverbs 6:27 to not be burned by the fire of immorality: **can a man rake together fire into his bosom and yet his very garments not be burned?** If you harden your heart to sexual images then you are going to miss the real love and real intimacy that you already have or that YHWH already has planned for you. Flee from sexual immorality. If you play with fire, you are going to get burned. If you look at porn then you can't be a Christian. A Christian loves YHWH. YHWH hates detestable things like pornography. The reason you can't stop looking at pornography is that you don't love YHWH enough. You are a faker.

Faker Christians tolerate homosexuality and other abnormal, unbiblical sexual relationships. Faker Christians tell others that living against biblical standards is acceptable. Some even go so far as to say that homosexuals can have the same rights and privileges in marriages. Some leaders in your church are blatant fornicators or tolerate other Christians who are living in sin, fornicating, or practicing adultery. Homosexuality is detestable to YHWH. (Leviticus 20:13) **And when a man lies down with a male the same as one lies down with a woman, both of them have done a detestable thing. They should be put to death without fail. Their own blood is upon them.** YHWH several other times in the bible states that homosexuality is a sin. Leviticus 18:22 and 1 Corinthians 6:9 are scriptures which say that homosexuality is detestable and that practicing homosexuals will not inherit the kingdom of God.

We cannot follow the second commandment at the expense of the first commandment. Jesus tells us in Mark 12:31 that the second most important commandment is **"Love your neighbor as yourself."** So love is always in order. But a sentence before that Jesus gives us the greatest commandment: **"you must love YHWH your God with your whole heart and with your whole soul and with your whole mind and with your whole strength."** We are told to put God first. That means we need to honor God and follow His rules. His rules, as outlined in His word, clearly state that sexual misconduct is a sin. Yes, we need to love others. But YHWH's standards must be kept. YHWH must always be first.

90% of homosexual behavior is learned. This is because it is cool to be homosexual these days. Women don't scream and gawk and chatter and use their hands and wrists as much as gay men. This overly flamboyant and stupid behavior is learned,

---

[3] http://www.covenanteyes.com/2013/02/19/pornography-statistics/

and is not a result of excessive estrogen. They flaunt their sinfulness in your face and are obsessed with sex and carnal desires, making those who genuinely have biological hormone disorders look bad.

Our hearts need to go out to those with genuine biological problems who, from birth, have always been attracted to those of the same sex. This is not part of God's plan just as being born with a disease and handicaps is not part of His plan. But sexuality is 1% of who we are, not 99% of who we are. So get over it. Homosexuality is a sin. A homosexual should never have sex. But guess what? Heterosexual sex outside of marriage is also a sin. So a heterosexual also has to conquer his sexual desires… or at least until the day he or she is married and able to express these desires within the confines of a biblical marriage. Many have to wait 30 or 40 years to find their wife or husband. Some never do. Straight or homosexual, you simply can't have sex until you are married. That means never for Homosexuals and perhaps years for a Heterosexual.

True Christians hate what is evil. Psalm 97:10 **O YOU lovers of YHWH, hate what is bad. He is guarding the souls of his loyal ones; Out of the hand of the wicked ones he delivers them.** If you love movies and books and magazines which don't honor YHWH, innuendos, coarse joking, magic, and sorcery then your choice of entertainment clearly shows that you are a part of this world and therefore aren't a real Christian.

Don't be like so many faker Christians out there who are like pigs who return to their slop.

(2 Peter 2: 22) **The saying of the true proverb has happened to them: "The dog has returned to its own vomit, and the sow that was bathed to rolling in the mire."** If you are unhappy with your life then seek YHWH and live your life in accordance with His principles. Living your life by YWHW's principles is the only source of peace and joy in this world. If you keep seeking comfort from the evil things of the world you are no better than a dog returning to his vomit.

<u>Time:</u> How long you spend being entertainment is also as important as how you are entertained. A good thing, in excess, can quickly turn into a bad thing. For example, e-mail and sharing pictures and staying connected with family is good up to the point when you go crazy if you don't have a WIFI connection and can't get onto your social networking site 10 times a day. Helping your kids develop is important up to the point when parents run themselves crazy to help their selfish kids, who don't even know about the God of the bible, become sport stars, piano stars, dance stars, club stars, and boy scouts. Video games can be fun and diverting up to the point when you spend too much time in them and your life becomes unbalanced.

Video games can be equally dangerous. Sadly there are people out there, predominantly boys, who live to play video games. These video gaming boys in men's bodies are so discouraged by reality that they seek refuge within the imaginary world of video games. Part of me can't blame them. At least video game friends won't lie to them and use them like real friends (please read the next chapter). Nonetheless, escaping from reality is not the way to endure and flourish in life. Please stop playing video games and seek the more important things. (Philippians 1:10)_ **That YOU may make sure of the more important things, so that YOU may be flawless and not be stumbling others up to the day of Christ.**

Violent video games are absolutely against YHWH's principal of sacrificially loving one another.

If you love violence, God hates you. Psalm 11:5-shows us that YHWH hates the person loving violence: **YHWH himself examines the righteous one as well as the wicked one, and anyone loving violence His soul certainly hates.** Wow those are strong words. YHWH hates you if you love violence, violent movies, or violent video games. Please think about this.

Sports can be fun but they can quickly become a huge distractor which takes you away from the more important priorities. In and of themselves, athletics and sports aren't bad. But too much of anything is almost always bad. It is such a shame that most men in Europe and the Americas know every statistic for their favorite football player or golfer but they don't have 3 scriptures memorized. Obviously these people are faker Christians. They go to church and claim to be Christians but on the inside they slap YHWH in the face by knowing more about their immoral, atheist sports hero than they do about any character in the bible.

Sports clothing is now tighter and more revealing than ever. What happened to Christian modesty and embarrassment? It is sad that men are so sinful that they have found a way to incorporate half naked women into every sporting event. It is sad that sporting events are all supported by women dressed inappropriately, cheering and dancing on the sidelines.

Go to a professional sports event and you can feel the collective energy of ignorant men worshiping the heroes of their soon to be forgotten lives. If only they would direct 10% of the passion they have for their favorite team towards learning more about and honoring their Grand Creator.

Too often people work for hours every day just to get that perfect physique to get attention or maintain self-esteem. This is wrong. Yet our bodies do require physical strength and health. As we get older we must be very deliberate about taking care of our bodies. We must spend a few hours a week, not each day, doing some type of physical activity. But we must have balance.

Inappropriate use of beverages, chemicals, and food are common forms of recreation which do not honor YHWH. Before we discuss these, we need to highlight a few bible scriptures which remind us the importance of our bodies.

Our bodies are temples of the Holy Spirit. (1 Corinthians 6:19-20) **"What! Do YOU not know that the body of YOU people is [the] temple of the holy spirit within YOU, which YOU have from God? Also, YOU do not belong to yourselves, for YOU were bought with a price. By all means, glorify God in the body of YOU people."**

We are told to offer our bodies as living sacrifices. (Romans 12:1-2) **"Consequently I entreat YOU by the compassions of God, brothers, to present YOUR bodies a sacrifice living, holy, acceptable to God, a sacred service with YOUR power of reason. And quit being fashioned after this system of things, but be transformed by making YOUR mind over, that YOU may prove to yourselves the good and acceptable and perfect will of God."**

Alcohol: All my Baptists associates imply that drinking alcohol is a reprehensible sin despite the fact that the bible makes countless references to the blessings of drinking wine. Jesus was called "gluttonous" and "given to drinking wine" (Matthew 11:19) so we can assume that he drank. We know that Jesus was sinless so drinking wine is not a sin. Self-righteous religious people of his times were only trying to slander him. In John 2: 1-11 we see at the marriage feast that Jesus did not just change water into wine, he changed it into "fine wine." This means Jesus knew the difference between quality and worthless wine.

Drunkenness is a sin. This is obvious. Let's look at the beginning of Isaiah for some strong scriptures about how YHWH sees drunkenness. YHWH warns us not to become drunks. (Isaiah 5:11) **Woe to those who are getting up early in the morning that they may seek just intoxicating liquor, who are lingering till late in the evening darkness so that wine itself inflames them!**

YHWH warns us not to take pride in drinking too much. (Isaiah 5:22) **Woe to those who are mighty in drinking wine, and to the men with vital energy for mixing intoxicating liquor.** It is interesting how YHWH uses the expression men with vital energy for mixing intoxicating liquor. That, among many things, is a reference to bar tenders. And of course that makes sense, because no true Christian would waste his life with a job where he served liquor to people (sad drunks at the local pub or glamorous movie stars at the en-vogue club) for money. Shame on you if you are a bar tender or drink too much or are a drunk or brag about your drinking tolerance or your ability to mix liquors. Those jobs and characteristics do not honor YHWH.

Smoking is a sin and if you smoke you are a faker Christian. Period. Don't roll your eyes. How gross it is to be walking through the doors of your church right before it starts and all the smokers are getting their last hit of nicotine before they go inside. You can't smoke a cigarette, which we all know kills you, and claim to be honoring the Holy Spirit within your body. Jesus tells us that the second most important commandment is to love our neighbor. (Mark 12:31) **The second is this, 'You must love your neighbor as yourself.' There is no other commandment greater than these."** Second hand smoke is proven to be worse than first hand smoke because it doesn't have a filter. How can you love your neighbor if you don't care about his lungs? What about parents who smoke in front of their kids and subject them to second hand smoke all day long?

To the faker Christian who smokes and pretends to follow the bible, please stop making Christians look bad. Please honor your body, a gift of the Holy Spirit, by not polluting it. Find something better to take your attention away from the worries of the day. Matthew 6:33-34 reminds us to **Keep on, then, seeking first the kingdom and his righteousness, and all these [other] things will be added to YOU. So, never be anxious about the next day, for the next day will have its own anxieties. Sufficient for each day is its own badness.**

Food: If we all agree that our bodies are temples of YHWH's power and that we want to honor Him with our bodies, then we must properly use food. YHWH loves food. Look at his generous creation. We are so blessed with yummy fruits and vegetables, and herbs, and meats. YHWH's imagination and generosity is unending. Psalm 34:8 implores us to "taste and see that YHWH is good." Jesus loved food. He always talked about figs, and wine, mustard seeds, fish. After his resurrection, Jesus even made barbeque fish for his disciples (John 21:9). Yet, too much or too little of anything can quickly become bad. And so now we must talk about obesity and eating disorders.

If you are so overweight that your health is in danger because you uncontrollably consume unhealthy food and beverages, then you are hurting your temple of the Holy Spirit. You are not investing your talents like a good servant but are wasting the investment that YHWH has made in you. Think of the millions of people with real handicaps who would love to have a healthy body with working limbs. And here you are with a normal, healthy body that has been so polluted that you are now dysfunctional. This is a sin. It is also possible that you feel bad about being overweight, and so you relieve your guilt by eating a lot of food, which feels good, only to make the problem worse. Food and guilt becomes a downward spiraling circle. You must prayerfully break this downward circle and let your body heal and become healthy. Luke 21:34 reminds us to not to overeat: **"But pay attention to yourselves that your hearts never become weighed down with overeating and heavy drinking and anxieties of life…"** Don't squander the gift YHWH has given you.

Not-eating is just as sinful. Being so worried about being skinny or fit has made so many people hurt their own bodies. Throwing up food or starving yourself or taking water pills or laxatives in order to become or remain skinny is a sin. Don't hurt your bodies like that. What a shock it would be if when you looked into the mirror what you saw was a reflection of your heart, not what the world sees. Your heart is the part of your body you need to make and keep beautiful. So please make your heart beautiful.

YHWH loves us and wants us to be happy. He gave us biblical principles to live by so that we can actually have happiness and joy. YHWH gave us a Sabbath so we can rest. He gave us wonderful food to enjoy. He created us with a desire to have fellowship and be social. He gave us a desire to have recreation and entertainment and music and laughter and joy. But Satan had perverted the world so much that most people wittingly or unwittingly partake of unwholesome and evil entertainment. Please reassess what you do for entertainment and how you do it.

And please be deliberate about the people with whom you enjoy your recreation. Doing good things with bad people can also be dangerous. Because soon enough, you will be doing bad things with these bad people.

6. Choose Your Friends Wisely

Church Hypocrisy / Tradition / Lie: Be friends with everyone.

Biblical Truth: YHWH wants you to be friends with your spiritual brothers and sisters, and to love, but do ministry to everyone else.

One of the biggest mistakes faker Christians make is that they are friends with everyone. Some fakers Christians have no problems having friends who are some of the dirtiest and most immoral people in the world. Other faker Christians befriend immoral people in the hope of eventually "saving them," but in the end become more like them. True Christians do what the bible says and the bible clearly says not to become worldly, not to become yoked together with unbelievers, and not to mix with people of other beliefs because they will tear you away from true worship of YHWH.

Let's look as some scriptures which show us how and with whom we should be friends.

Friendship with the world is enmity with God. (James 4:4) **Adulteresses, do YOU not know that the friendship with the world is enmity with God? Whoever, therefore, wants to be a friend of the world constitutes himself an enemy of God.** This is a very strong scripture. We are not supposed to be friends with the world. We should not enjoy the fleeting and dying temporary joys of the world. We should not be lusting after the privileges and the riches and power and sin of the world.

A real Christian is not fashioned after the world. (Romans 12:1-2) **Consequently I entreat YOU by the compassions of God, brothers, to present YOUR bodies a sacrifice living, holy, acceptable to God, a sacred service with YOUR power of reason. And quit being fashioned after this system of things, but be transformed by making YOUR mind over, that YOU may prove to yourselves the good and acceptable and perfect will of God.** We are encouraged not to look (figuratively and literally) like the world.

Bad company corrupts good character. (1 Corinthians 15:33) **Do not be misled. Bad associations spoil useful habits.** What a clear scripture, so easy to understand. If you hang out with bad associates, all of your useful habits or character will be spoiled.

Perhaps there is wisdom in the non-scriptural proverb "show me who your friends are and I will show you who you are." This is a concept I frequently think about with regards to my son and daughter. Since they are still young and are so impressionable, my wife and I are always concerned about who their friends are and what type of influence they are. And since the majority of the world could care less about YHWH, it is more and more difficult to find the right kind of friends.

If you spend time with unwise people you will regret it. (Proverbs 13:20)-**He that is walking with wise persons will become wise, but he that is having dealings with the stupid ones will fare badly.**

All people in your life should fall into 2 categories:

1) Those <u>who</u> encourage you to be more like Jesus and glorify YHWH in accordance with biblical principles and
2) Those <u>who do not</u> encourage you to be more like Jesus and glorify YHWH in accordance with biblical principles.

Let's simplify this dichotomy by labeling them good associates and bad associates.

It is good for you to become friends with good associates. It is foolish to become friends with bad associates. The bible makes it clear that good associates can become friends and bad associates must be ministry opportunities.

So the question becomes how should I interact with bad associates? The answer is to be **"salt"** and **"light"** (Matthew 5:13 & 14). But being salt and light doesn't mean tolerating their sinful behavior. You must do ministry, not hint at or give approval to their unbiblical lives.

I know so many faker Christians who are friends with bad associates and call it "being a good example" to them. The problem is that being a good example is not enough. Ministry includes honest, but loving, words of truth.

Many faker Christians justify the fact that their friends are bad associates by saying that Jesus also hung out with sinners. First of all, you are not Jesus. You are not perfect. You can't read or know people's hearts and minds. Secondly, you don't understand the scriptures and need to reread all the gospels. Jesus did not hang out with sinners. Jesus hung out with repentant sinners who were seeking the truth and the Kingdom of God.

Yes, Jesus did run into sinners. Example one is the woman at the well who had five husbands (John 4). She was a sinner. Jesus didn't say "hey lets hang out and be friends. It is ok that you have had five husbands and obviously don't respect YHWH or His plan for sacred marriage." Jesus mentioned her husbands, which must have reminded the woman of her own sin. After Jesus got done telling her how modern religious leaders were off in their understanding of worship, He said that one day

"true worshipers will worship the Father with spirit and truth, for, indeed, the Father is looking for such like ones to worship him. God is a Spirit, and those worshiping him must worship with spirit and truth" (John 4:23-24).

The woman then went and told everyone about what she learned and who she found. You can read the story in John 4, but let me summarize. Jesus meets a sinful woman. Jesus lovingly reminds her that what she is doing is a sin. He then talks about true worship. The sinful woman tells many in the City. They go listen to Jesus. Many believe.

Another example of Jesus being around a sinner is when he eats with Zacchaeus the tax collector in Luke 19: 1-10. Zacchaeus ends up repenting, changing his heart and his behavior, gives ½ his belongings to the poor and he says he will repay fourfold anyone who he has cheated. Obviously this man was repentant and was working to right the wrongs of his life before coming into the truth.

Jesus' last sentence to Zacchaeus gives us some insight into how to relate to sinners. Jesus came to save, not to befriend. (Luke 19:10) **For the Son of man came to seek and to save what was lost.**

Saving those who are lost means bringing them out of danger. If you want to save a person from falling off a cliff you have to show them the cliff and pull them away from the cliff. If you don't point out what the cliff is and how it is dangerous, they will just go back to the cliff and fall off it once you leave. Similarly, if you want to save someone from death and destruction you have to let them know the sins they are committing and how they need to avoid that sin. It is loving to ask if you can help someone change their life for the glory of YHWH but they will likely never change if you don't remind them that their behavior is unacceptable in the eyes of YHWH. This is why it is important to do ministry, not become friends with those whose actions slap God in the face every day.

Having the wrong kind of "friends" can be dangerous. Let's say for example that you have a friend from work who is a homosexual. You like to spend time together playing sports. You eventually become good friends. One day you ask this man to babysit your little boy and this man molests him. Of course molesting children is evil. But make no mistake about it, the guilty one is the father who let a homosexual be alone with his son. A practicing homosexual is already outside of the will of God. A practicing homosexual has demonstrated that he practices abnormal sexual perversions. How dare you let someone who slaps God in the face and who is a sexual deviant be alone with your child.

Read the story of Dinah in the Genesis 33-34 to see an example of a Hebrew girl who made friends with the wrong people and who eventually was raped. Dinah's brother revenged themselves and many people were killed. The consequences of Dinah associating herself with worldly people were devastating.

Let's take a less extreme example which is just as serious. You like to share recreation activities with the couple next door. They are atheists. You have invited them to church about 10 times but they have refused because they don't believe in God. Why in the world would you want to be friends with someone who slaps YHWH in the face every day by refusing to believe in Him? Romans 1:20 reminds us that God's signature on the glorious art of His creation is so obvious that man is excuseless.

Romans 1:18 reminds us that YHWH's wrath will be revealed against people like your atheist neighbors who don't believe in Him. (Romans 1:18-20)-**For God's wrath is being revealed from heaven against all ungodliness and unrighteousness of men who are suppressing the truth in an unrighteous way, because what may be known about God is manifest among them, for God made it manifest to them. For his invisible [qualities] are clearly seen from the world's creation onward, because they are perceived by the things made, even his eternal power and Godship, so that they are inexcusable.**

You should love your neighbor. You should try to tell them the truth. You should teach them about YHWH, the Kingdom of God, and the ransom sacrifice of His wonderful son. But they must never be your friends until they change and live their lives in accordance with biblical principles. And if they never do, then they never become your friends and you have the privilege to love them as neighbors, not as friends.

Another example: Your teenage daughter or son comes home with a group of disrespectful kids who smell like marijuana, curse, dress like slobs or gangster rappers or prostitutes, and have their faces hidden behind their smart cell phones like antisocial misfits. But your child tells you they are the "popular kids" at school. Are you going to let them into your house and let them influence your family? You are not wise if you do.

Worse yet, why are you, full grown adults who claim to be Christians, chasing after the "popular people" of this evil world in an attempt to be like them, look like them, and be their friends. Think about it. Are you any better than a dumb teenage boy who just wants to be popular? A godly child knows she is loved by the creator of the Universe and only wants to glorify Him. A godly child doesn't want to be liked by the "popular people" who are stars in Satan's world. A godly child wants to be friends with like-minded people who love and honor God.

We should not accept or require praise from our fellow man. We should only seek YHWH's approval. Many faker Christians are just as bad as the people of the world in that they are lonely and insecure and will put up with anyone as long as they get attention. This is why girls have boyfriends who beat them. This is why peer pressure gets kids to have premarital sex, smoke, use drugs. If you only cared about making YHWH happy, then you wouldn't put up with the ridiculous behavior of people of this world. Jesus sets us straight by saying that we should not accept glory from men. (John 5:41) **I do not accept glory from men.**

A true friend is so likeminded and loving that in the bible he is compared to a brother. (Proverbs 18: 24) **There exist companions disposed to break one another to pieces, but there exists a friend sticking closer than a brother.**

Spending time with bad people is not biblical. That means you should not hang out with trouble makers from work at their Christmas parties, at their birthday parties, social events, and sporting events. Your time is your life and a true Christian won't waste it with people who dishonor YHWH.

Loving YHWH means doing what He says. (John 14:15) **If YOU love me, YOU will observe my commandments.**

Jesus didn't like those who ignored God for the sake of human traditions. (Matthew 15:3) **In reply he said to them: Why is it YOU also overstep the commandment of God because of YOUR tradition?**

Honor God with your Heart, not just your lips. (Matthew 15: 6-9) **And so YOU have made the word of God invalid because of YOUR tradition. YOU hypocrites, Isaiah aptly prophesied about YOU, when he said, This people honors me with their lips, yet their heart is far removed from me. It is in vain that they keep worshiping me, because they teach commands of men as doctrines.**

Obedience is important. One of the benefits of obedience is that God gives Holy Spirit to the obedient. (Acts 5:32) **And we are witnesses of these matters, and so is the holy spirit, which God has given to those obeying him as ruler.**

The bible clearly says not to become yoked together with unbelievers and not to mix with people of other beliefs because they will tear you away from true worship of YHWH. Now that we have discussed how a true Christian relates to friends and neighbors, let's look at how true Christians should relate to the world in general.

7. Christians should not be a part of this World

Church Hypocrisy / Tradition / Lie: Look like everyone else in the world, but come to church on Sunday.

Biblical Truth: Godly people are not part of this world.

Many people think that Christians can't be "cool." That is absolutely right. If you are "cool" then you are a part of the systems of the world. And this system of things is evil. If you want to be "cool" then you are seeking the approval of people in the world and not the approval of your Father in heaven.

Faker Christians all over the world look just like the people of the world. But if you actually believe the scriptures and do what they say, then your life will be marked by holiness and love and you will stick out from the world.

True Christians are not supposed to be fashioned by the world. (Romans 12:1) **and quit being fashioned after this system of things, but be transformed by making YOUR mind over, that YOU may prove to yourselves the good and acceptable and perfect will of God.**

The reason we don't want to be fashioned by worldly systems is that the world is lying in the power of Satan. (1 John 5:19) **We know we originate with God, but the whole world is lying in the [power of the] wicked one.**

Friendship with the World is Enmity with God. (James 4:4) **Adulteresses, do YOU not know that the friendship with the world is enmity with God? Whoever, therefore, wants to be a friend of the world is constituting himself an enemy of God.**

Jesus was not part of this world and said in his famous John 17 prayer that his followers would also not be a part of this world. (John 17:16) **They are no part of the world, just as I am no part of the world.**

When they tried to make Jesus a political leader, a king from the line of David, Jesus left them. His kingdom is not of this world. Jesus was not political. (John 6:15) **Therefore Jesus, knowing they were about to come and seize him to make him king, withdrew again into the mountain all alone.**

The men in leadership positions in worldly organizations are ambitious and care nothing (they are fakers) for the will of YHWH. Christian chaplains and many catholic priests forget their "calling" and that their purpose is to love and serve GOD

ALMIGHTY, not get promoted and make money. Political leaders are inundated with sex scandals and lies and controversies. Look at how incompetent our military senior leaders are. Look at how evil and selfish CEOs are who ruin companies or banks, costing tax payers billions of dollars, crashing economies as a result. If you want to be a friend of the world then you are not a friend of God.

Only a few times in all of bible history did YHWH raise up a "believing insider" from a worldly government. Joseph became a leader in Egypt to help the Israelites find food and safety. Moses was trained by Pharaoh but eventually help the Israelites escape. Based off of Jesus' example to flee from those who want him to be political, we can see that for 99.9999999% of all men (which means the exception is not you) any one serving God Almighty should be apolitical.

You can serve only one master so it better be YHWH. (Matthew 6:24) **"No one can slave for two masters; for either he will hate the one and love the other, or he will stick to the one and despise the other. YOU cannot slave for God and for Riches.**

Let's see an example of how this applies to modern day life. A faker Christian wants to make a difference in the world so he joins the military of one of the corrupt governments of this world and serves as a chaplain. He prays for soldiers who go off to war in support of that nation's objectives. This faker chaplain would never have the courage to give "tough-love" and to speak the words of God. He would likely do his best to be politically correct. This faker chaplain is likely as ambitious and as concerned about advancing in rank as the average atheist infantry officer to whom he volunteered to minister. This faker chaplain knows stories of the bible like a well-educated child but doesn't live in accordance with biblical truths. This faker Christian supports his nation at the cost of watering down the truth of the scriptures.

This faker Christian chaplain feels like he is bold when he says "and I pray this in Jesus' name" and yet is such a faker that he doesn't even know or use or try to glorify the name of YHWH. And if he does know the name of YHWH, he is way too afraid to ever say it in public. That would be a career ender for sure. Do you see how working for a government is impossible if you truly love YHWH and want to live in accordance with His principles?

Now let's imagine a civil war-one like the US Civil War. Just think about hypocritical Baptist chaplains in New York who prayed for God to bless their soldiers as they went off to kill their literal brothers from Virginia. Just think about hypocritical Baptist chaplains in Virginia who prayed for God to bless their soldiers as they went off to kill their literal brothers from New York.

How about an international example? Just think of Lutheran chaplains in Germany praying for God to bless their soldiers as they went off to kill Americans. Or just think of Lutheran chaplains in the USA praying for God to bless their soldiers as they went off to kill Germans. In the last 200 years the only Christian denomination which has never taken up arms against their brothers is Jehovah's Witnesses. Every other denomination presumes to be fighting on God's side and takes up weapons against other Christian brothers who also wrongly assume they are on God's side. Who decides which side has God's blessing?

Exiled Israelites did not join the military of their captors and fight to support their causes. Take Jeremiah for example. After the Babylonians destroyed Jerusalem did Jeremiah move to Iraq and volunteer to fight for the Babylonians? Of course not. His identity as a child of the living God, an Israelite, required that he stay loyal to YHWH, not the king of Babylon, Persia, Greece, or Caesar. Jesus's followers did not join the Roman military to fight for Caesar. They remained politically neutral.

Now let's see what a modern, real Man of God would do. He would be apolitical, he would be neutral. He would be clean and loving and not look like the world. If given an opportunity to speak with someone serving in the military, he would lovingly tell them the good news about the Kingdom of God, ask if he could help that soldier come into an accurate knowledge of YHWH and live in accordance with biblical principles. A real Man of God would never wear a uniform which has the flag of a nation which kills and aborts over a million babies a year, spends billions of dollars a year waging war or making weapons of war, and continually slaps YHWH in the face by legalizing homosexual marriages and claiming on their money that "In God We Trust."

But what about Christians from another country, say for example China? Collectively, the Chinese are just as evil as any other world power, but in different ways. They don't value life, kill babies, eat dogs, aggressively suppress freedom of speech and religion, worship false oriental gods, and have extreme socio-economic polarity. What about a Muslim country like Turkey, Syria? A Christian in China or Turkey or Syria can't join the military and kill people to support their nation's "evil" way of life. A Christian can't join the Chinese or Turkish or Syrian government and support such a corrupt political system. Regardless of where you live, as a Christian you must remain neutral, mind your own business, pay taxes, obey the speed limit, and be a law abiding citizen. But your loyalty but be to YHWH. A real Man of God knows that our lying, dishonorable world leaders are absolutely outside the will of YHWH and not worthy of our service.

Neutral real Christians only seek the approval of YHWH, not men. (John 5:41)-**I do not accept glory from men.**

If you vote or sign a petition it would be as if you were saying that human governments or leadership can solve the world's problems. The only solution to the world's problems is YHWH's Kingdom.

Because we all live in a country, and every country has rules, we must obey those rules as long as they don't conflict with biblical principles. We must pay taxes, obey the speed limit and so on. But that doesn't mean we have to approve of and participate in wars, political parties, immoral cultural norms. Give to Caesar what is Caesar's. (Mark 12:17) **Jesus then said: "Pay back Caesar's things to Caesar, but God's things to God."**

The world is a sinking ship and it would be a waste of time trying to become the captain of that ship. Spending time rearranging chairs and making your bed on the Titanic was a waste of time. It is the same for the world. Working for governments which are not the solution to man's problems is a waste of time because the world is passing away. What we do and what we spend our time doing must be of lasting value. What we do must make YHWH happy.

OK. Let's be reasonable. What does someone do if they love God and want to help make the world a better place?

What we must do is what Jesus commissioned his disciples to do. (Matthew 28:18-20) **And Jesus approached and spoke to them, saying: "All authority has been given me in heaven and on the earth. Go therefore and make disciples of people of all the nations, baptizing them in the name of the Father and of the Son and of the holy spirit, teaching them to observe all the things I have commanded YOU."**

The world is passing away so do the will of YHWH in order to live forever. (1 John 2:15-17) **Do not be loving either the world or the things in the world. If anyone loves the world, the love of the Father is not in him; because everything in the world—the desire of the flesh and the desire of the eyes and the showy display of one's means of life—does not originate with the Father, but originates with the world. Furthermore, the world is passing away and so is its desire, but he that does the will of God remains forever.**

Jesus was perfect and obviously could have been the greatest king to ever rule in Israel. Yet he didn't want to be a part of the systems of this world. He knew the world was passing away. Jesus knew that the only solution is God's Kingdom. That is why Jesus prayed for YHWH's kingdom to come in His model prayer. (Matthew 6:9-10) **"YOU must pray, then, this way: "Our Father in the heavens, let your name be**

sanctified. Let your kingdom come. Let your will take place, as in heaven, also upon earth."

A real Christian should be like Jesus and wait for God's Kingdom to come. We should not serve human governments which have no chance for success. We should love YHWH with our all and love our neighbor as ourselves. We should make disciples of men and teach them to observe the things that YHWH commanded.

The bible says we can't serve two masters (Matthew 6:24). So we must serve YHWH, not the world. We must worship YHWH, not money. Our next chapter will illustrate how the hypocritical church has turned from worshiping YHWH to serving the god of money.

8. Most Churches are Dens of Thieves not Houses of Prayer

Church Hypocrisy / Tradition / Lie: Make money from spiritual things. Charge for services rendered. Accessorize.

Biblical Truth: God doesn't want you to make knowing Him into a money making business opportunity.

YHWH made the world in six days. Can the creator of the universe who made the Northern Lights (Aurora Borealis) or countless colorful galaxies or the Swiss Alps or Grand Canyon be confined to a brick structure made by human hands? Obviously the answer is "NO."

Does God need your money? The answer is also "NO." Yet, YHWH is reasonable and knows that humans these days need provisions (food, clothing, shelter..) for survival. When His servants needed money in the past, YHWH always provided. They never had to have a bake sale, an auction, sell bricks, sell candles, sell forgiveness of sins, pass a plate, or make automatic bank account deductions.

YHWH provides: The Egyptians gave the Israelites gold and valuable when they left Egypt (Exodus 12:36). The gold brought to Mary and Joseph by the astrologers possibly finances their time of refuge in Egypt while Herod was killing all the children in Bethlehem (Matthew 2:11-15).

If YHWH wants something to happen, He will make it happen. (Isaiah 55:11) **so my word that goes forth from my mouth will prove to be. It will not return to me without results, but it will certainly do that in which I have delighted, and it will have certain success in that for which I have sent it.**

Faker Christians and their churches and denominations love to make money off of anything spiritual. This is one reason that the faker Christian churches have been led astray. (1 Timothy 6: 9-10) **However, those who are determined to be rich fall into temptation and a snare and many senseless and hurtful desires, which plunge men into destruction and ruin. For the love of money is a root of all sorts of injurious things, and by reaching out for this love some have been led astray from the faith and have stabbed themselves all over with many pains.**

Micah prophesied about the corruption of faker Christian churches which accept bribes and charge for their services. (Micah 3:11) **Her leaders judge for a bribe, Her priests instruct for a price, And her prophets practice divination for money. And yet they lean on YHWH, saying: "Is not YHWH with us No calamity will**

come upon us." How much does your priest charge you to conduct a marriage ceremony or funeral? How much did you pay to go to a bible seminar or retreat? Instructing for a price is not biblical.

You can't serve two masters. (Matthew 6:24) **"No one can slave for two masters; for either he will hate the one and love the other, or he will stick to the one and despise the other. YOU cannot slave for God and for Riches.**

Don't store up treasures on earth. (Matthew 6: 19-21) **"Stop storing up for yourselves treasures upon the earth, where moth and rust consume, and where thieves break in and steal. Rather, store up for yourselves treasures in heaven, where neither moth nor rust consumes, and where thieves do not break in and steal. For where your treasure is, there your heart will be also".**

Jesus particularly did not like faker religious leaders who turned things of god into money making ventures. (Mark 11:15-17) **Now they came to Jerusalem. There he entered into the temple and started to throw out those selling and buying in the temple, and he overturned the tables of the money changers and the benches of those selling doves; and he would not let anyone carry a utensil through the temple, but he kept teaching and saying: "Is it not written, 'My house will be called a house of prayer for all the nations'? But YOU have made it a cave of robbers."**

The angriest account of Jesus recorded in the bible is when he flips the table and accuses the fakers of turning a house or prayer into a den of thieves. This should tell you something. Jesus, who is a perfect reflection of YHWH, gets the most upset at people taking advantage of the people for financial gain.

Some catholic and protestant cathedrals charge entrance fees. This is in violation of biblical principles and turns the cathedral into a den of thieves.

It is impossible to enter into a catholic church in Europe which doesn't have candles for sale. Most cathedrals now have an entire corner where they sell books, post cards, stamped euros or pennies, rosaries and crosses. These gift shops are in violation of biblical principles and turn the church into a den of thieves.

I remember taking my family to the famous cathedral in Canterbury, England. They were charging a $15 per person entrance fee. My teenage daughter and I got a bit grumpy at this hypocrisy. Perhaps that is why we usually write things like "a $15 entrance fee is absurd. Please read Mark 11:17" on the guest registers at churches like this. Speaking of the Canterbury cathedral, it is a perfect example of a church which promoted war and patriotism and encouraged Great Britain during their bloody and money hungry quest to take over the world. Remember that at one point in time, the sun never set on the British Empire. The cathedral is full of dead kings and warriors and flags and war banners. They obviously didn't read the scriptures sited in the previous chapter about Christians not being a part of this world and how they are supposed to love God and their neighbors until God's kingdom finally comes.

The Catholic Church used to sell "indulgences" to pay for their luxurious living and grand buildings. A rich man could buy forgiveness. How revolting and satanic and unbiblical. Although the sale of indulgences is no longer practiced formally, modern day church leaders frequently prostitute themselves to the rich and powerful. This is in violation of biblical principles and turns the church into a den of thieves.

It costs money to get married in most modern day churches. This is in violation of biblical principles and turns the church into a den of thieves.

Buying a faker Christian book at the local book store or Christian book store costs as much as buying a secular book. That is because the faker Christian book companies are only interested in making money. They simply use faker Christian book sales as their means of making money.

If you really believe that what you were writing has the hope of changing a person's eternal destiny then you would make it available for free, or in my case, simply cover the cost of printing the book.

All faker Christian book authors are hypocrites who do not live in accordance with biblical principles. Disgusting faker Christian ministers flash money around and pervert and twist the scriptures to make you believe that if YHWH loves you, you will be rich. The "prosperity gospel" is a lie from Satan and it doesn't matter if you have a mega church in a football stadium, you are outside the will of YHWH.

Faker Christians who say we should pray for riches like Jabez in 1 Chronicles 4:10 ought to read the rest of the bible which says the first will be last, love our neighbor, keep your eye simple, seek first the kingdom, make disciples of all men, love YHWH with your all, and put others first. Shame on you who say and publish these unbiblical lies.

Think of the most famous evangelizers or apologists or want to be youth role models making millions of dollars via their world-wide ministries. One claims to have the gift of healing yet can't fix his own back. He dyes his hair gray to look mature and wise and his wife, who has had countless surgeries and implants, travels with him only to ensure he remains sexually faithful? Is that the way a godly man loves and supports his wife? What about another popular Christian rock star who commercialized "sexual purity" yet was a lying hypocrite? Is that the way a godly woman behaves?

How sad it is that so many have made millions of dollars off of lies. This is in violation of biblical principles and turns their ministries into a den of thieves.

Jesus tells us the standard for Christian ministry. (Matthew 10: 8) **YOU received free, give free.**

Bible publishers, if you actually believe that the Word of God is living and active you should do your best to provide it for free or at cost. Most of you are satanic publishing companies which only want to make money. Shame on you!

When I was a faker Christian, I read Zondervan's New International Version several times. As I began to have my eyes opened to biblical truths it became obvious that Zondervan is run by faker Christians who hide the name of YHWH and who charge way too much for the precious and life changing word of God. If you have printed millions of copies then the overhead costs must become very, very low. How sad that you keep the rights to your poor translation. Shame on you for charging almost a hundred dollars for a copy of the King James Bible with references to Greek and Hebrew words. The Strong's Concordance was written over a hundred years ago. You should charge six or seven dollars for the paper and leather, not 80 dollars. Meditate on Matthew 10: 8 **"YOU received free, give free."** All people want to do is look up the original Greek or Hebrew word in order to better understand the truth. If you actually believe the word of God is living and active then you should stop focusing on selling the bible to English speakers and would try to help translate the bible into many other languages to reach the lost sheep.

If you actually believe that the word of God is inspired then you must believe that the Catholic Bible is not inspired. Why in the world would a publishing company publish and sell the inspired bible and also publish and sell the uninspired bible? You are fakers and your goal is money, not the Kingdom. Your organization is a den of thieves and shame on you for making money off of the inspired word of God.

Like many other religious organizations, the Vatican is a den of thieves. In some European nations, if you claim to be catholic, then a certain percentage of your wages are garnished and are electronically transferred each month to the Vatican's bank account. This is Nauseating!

How many people know about all the financial investments, properties, and businesses of the Vatican? Jesus and Paul and Peter worked hard until the day they were killed for the sake of the Kingdom of God. How much money does a local priest get for his retirement? How much money does a retired bishop get for his retirement?

What about the last pope Benedict who left in shame, after having been caught in a scandal, disgracing the name of god to all who associate YHWH with your faker Christian organization. Shame on the Vatican? How much money a month is that criminal getting for his retirement? The Vatican is not a representative of YHWH. It is a money making machine. No wonder the kings of the earth commit fornication with you (Revelations 18:10). No wonder the merchants of the world will be sad to see your destruction (Revelations 18:11). What you do is in violation of biblical principles and reveals your catholic church to be a den of thieves.

Salaries: YHWH's faithful servants work out of love, not for huge salaries. Jesus warns us of shepherds who are paid and only work for money. (John 10:12) **The hired man, who is no shepherd and to whom the sheep do not belong as his own, beholds the wolf coming and abandons the sheep and flees—and the wolf snatches them and scatters them.**

YHWH deserves those who will worship Him in spirit and truth. True Christians do their best to mitigate costs and do everything and give everything for free. They give their lives to the Kingdom of God. True Christians would never force money collections, charge for services, charge for spiritual truths, charge for literature, charge for bibles, and make you pay to attend a spiritual conference. Jesus reminds us that the standard for Christian ministry is "free." (Matthew 10:8) **"YOU received free, give free."**

Making money off of God's word and the good news of God's Kingdom is a hypocritical tradition of faker Christians. Let's now move on to other unbiblical and hypocritical traditions of the church: the nature of Jesus and the trinity.

9. Jesus is 1st Born of Creation

Church Hypocrisy / Tradition / Lie: Jesus is God.

Biblical Truth: Jesus is YHWH's son, the firstborn of all creation who helped YHWH make all things, who came to earth to give us a perfect example and to die as our ransom. He is now at the right hand of the Father, has been delegated all authority, will judge the living and the dead, and will rule as the King of Kings in the Kingdom of God.

Jesus is YHWH's son. (Matthew 3:17) **Look! Also, a voice from the heavens said: "This is my Son, the beloved, whom I have approved"**

Jesus is the firstborn of all creation who helped YHWH make all things. (Colossians 1:15-16) **He is the image of the invisible God, the firstborn of all creation; because by means of him all other things were created in the heavens and on the earth, the things visible and the things invisible, whether they are thrones or lordships or governments or authorities. All other things have been created through him and for him.**

Jesus came to earth to give us a perfect example. (1 Peter 2: 21) **In fact, to this course you were called, because even Christ suffered for you, leaving a model for you to follow his steps closely.**

Jesus is our ransom. (1 Timothy 2: 5-6) **For there is one God, and one mediator between God and men, a man, Christ Jesus, who gave himself a corresponding ransom for all—this is what is to be witnessed to in its own due time.**

Jesus is now at the right hand of the Father. (1 Peter 3:22) **He is at God's right hand, for he went to heaven, and angels and authorities and powers were made subject to him.**

Jesus has been delegated all authority. (Matthew 28:18) **Jesus approached and spoke to them, saying: "All authority has been given me in heaven and on the earth."**

Jesus will judge the living and the dead. (2 Timothy 4:1-22) **"I solemnly charge you before God and Christ Jesus, who is destined to judge the living and the dead, and by his manifestation and his kingdom, preach the word, be at it urgently in favorable season, in troublesome season, reprove, reprimand, exhort, with all long-suffering and [art of] teaching."**

Jesus will rule as the King of Kings in the Kingdom of God. (Revelation 19:16) **On his outer garment, yes, on his thigh, he has a name written, King of kings and Lord of lords.**

As YHWH's master builder, Jesus helped design and bring into creation all the thousands of yummy fruits and vegetables. Of course Jesus took advantage of his 33 years on earth to enjoy the delicious flavors of life. (Psalms 34:8) **Taste and see that YHWH is good.**

Look at the references to pomegranates and figs and wine and vines and vineyards and milk and honey and sweet cakes throughout the bible. YHWH and Jesus created a world that was spectacularly enjoyable. Thank you, Father.

While on earth, Jesus loved the delicious varieties of creation so much so that his opponents even called him a glutton. (Luke 7: 34-35) **The Son of man has come eating and drinking, but you say: 'Look! A man who is a glutton and is given to drinking wine, a friend of tax collectors and sinners!' All the same, wisdom is proved righteous by all its children."**

Jesus was loved. Even the kids like to be with him. One great example of Jesus' character was the way Jesus was silly, yet obedient, with his mother at the Cana wedding. (John 2:4) **But Jesus said to her: "Woman, why is that of concern to me and to you? My hour has not yet come."**

Jesus is like YHWH. (John 14:6-7) **Jesus said to him: "I am the way and the truth and the life. No one comes to the Father except through me. If you men had known me, you would have known my Father also; from this moment on you know him and have seen him."**

Jesus was the most courageous person to ever live. Imagine the courage it takes to tell the faker religious hypocrites that they are working for Satan. In John 8:44, Jesus said to them: **"You are from your father the Devil, and you wish to do the desires of your father."**

As the righteous judge, Jesus will prevent so many people from inheriting everlasting life. This means Jesus will say "No" to billions of people who did not prioritize honoring YHWH. (Matthew 7:21-23) **"Not everyone saying to me, 'Lord, Lord,' will enter into the kingdom of the heavens, but the one doing the will of my Father who is in the heavens will. Many will say to me in that day, 'Lord, Lord, did we not prophesy in your name, and expel demons in your name, and perform many powerful works in your name?' And yet then I will confess to them: I never knew YOU! Get away from me, YOU workers of lawlessness."**

Come, Lord Jesus. (Revelation 22:20) **"Amen! Come, Lord Jesus."**

10. The "Trinity" is not in the Bible

Church Hypocrisy / Tradition / Lie: The Holy Spirit is God. Jesus is God.

Biblical Truth: There is only one God in the world and YHWH is His name. Jesus is His son and "holy spirit" is another way to describe YHWH's power.

YHWH is one, not THREE! (Deuteronomy 6:4) **Listen, O Israel: YHWH our God is <u>one</u> YHWH.**

There is no such thing as the trinity.

The term trinity is not even in the bible.

Jesus is not YHWH but is YHWH's first born of creation, His son.

Holy spirit is not YHWH but is another way of saying "YHWH's power."

YHWH doesn't like confusion, disorder. (1 Corinthians 14:33) **For God is [a God], not of disorder, but of peace.**

Being a God of order, He would never want to make himself a "mystery," confusing, or unknowable. It is sad when the church says that the trinity is a "mystery," that father, son, and spirit are all the same substance, three in one, and that sometimes the parts act together and other times they act independently. This is nonsense.

Jesus was not schizophrenic. When he prayed, he did not pray to himself but prayed to YHWH, his father. (John 17: 1-3) **Jesus spoke these things, and, raising his eyes to heaven, he said: "Father, the hour has come; glorify your son, that your son may glorify you, according as you have given him authority over all flesh, that, as regards the whole [number] whom you have given him, he may give them everlasting life. This means everlasting life, their taking in knowledge of you, the only true God, and of the one whom you sent forth, Jesus Christ.**

Jesus taught us to pray to YHWH. (Matthew 6:9) **"YOU must pray, then, this way: "'Our Father in the heavens let your name be sanctified.**

Solomon tells us that Jesus is different from YHWH. (Proverbs 30:4) **Who has ascended to heaven and then descended? Who has gathered the wind in the palms of both hands? Who has wrapped up the waters in his garment? Who has established all the ends of the earth? What is his name and the name of his son—if you know?**

Many pagan cultures had ideas of the three gods. The Egyptians had a "big three" of their false gods. The Greeks also had a top three. It is easy to see in history how the faker catholic church adopted this idea of three in one to appease the pagans to bring them into the church.

YHWH shares his glory with no one, not even Jesus. (Isaiah 42:8) **I am YHWH. That is my name; and to no one else shall I give my own glory, neither my praise to graven images.**

YHWH's power (holy spirit) has no name. If they were three personalities in one, then the holy spirit would have a name. But the holy spirit doesn't have a name because the holy spirit is not a person but is a way of describing YHWH's power.

YHWH's power (holy spirit) isn't a person. Stephen is given a glimpse of the throne room of YHWH and sees Jesus at his right hand. But he never sees a 3rd person of the holy spirit (Acts 7: 55-56) This is because holy spirit is simply just a way of describing YHWH's power.

YHWH's power (holy spirit) doesn't have its own personality. YHWH's power is translated as a **"helper"** (John 14:16), or the **"spirit of Truth"** (John 16:13). This does not mean that holy spirit has a mind of its own. It simply reveals that YHWH's power helps people.

Jesus and his father were / are distinct. (Matthew 26:39) **And going a little way forward, he fell upon his face, praying and saying: "My Father, if it is possible, let this cup pass away from me. Yet, not as I will, but as you will."** If Jesus was in a trinity then why would he schizophrenically pray to himself? He prayed to his father because his father, YHWH, is superior.

Jesus is not part of a false trinity but is subordinate to YHWH. (1 Corinthians 11:3) **But I want YOU to know that the head of every man is the Christ; in turn the head of a woman is the man; in turn the head of the Christ is God.**

Jesus was not eternal like YHWH but was made by YHWH. (Colossians 1:15) **He is the image of the invisible God, the firstborn of all creation.**

There is only one God and his name is YHWH, not Jesus. YHWH is the only God. All else are fake gods and false gods. (Isaiah 45: 5) **I am YHWH, and there is no one else. With the exception of me there is no God.**

Because YHWH delegated to Jesus many powers, Jesus was powerful and was described as "a" god in John 1:1 but not "the" God. (John 1:1-2) **In the beginning the Word was, and the Word was with God, and the Word was a god. This one was**

in the beginning with God. Many Greek scholars translate John 1:1 as the Word (Jesus) was "a" god, using the definite article "A." About the same amount of Greek scholars translate John 1:1 as the Word was god, without using the indefinite article "A." If you use the term "a god" then it makes sense because we all know the amazing powers YHWH delegated to Jesus made Jesus "god like."

Jesus was delegated powers which made him "god like" but Jesus never considered himself equal to YHWH. (Philippians 2:5-8) **Keep this mental attitude in YOU that was also in Christ Jesus, who, although he was existing in God's form, gave no consideration to a seizure, namely, that he should be equal to God. No, but he emptied himself and took a slave's form and came to be in the likeness of men. More than that, when he found himself in fashion as a man, he humbled himself and became obedient as far as death, yes, death on a torture stake.**

There may be those who are "god like" but there is only one God, YHWH. (1 Corinthians 8:5-6) **For even though there are those who are called "gods," whether in heaven or on earth, just as there are many "gods" and many "lords," there is actually to us one God the Father, out of whom all things are, and we for him; and there is one Lord, Jesus Christ, through whom all things are, and we through him.**

Moses was just a man and yet YHWH called him "God to Pharaoh". Exodus 7:1 **Consequently YHWH said to Moses: "See, I have made you God to Pharaoh, and Aaron your own brother will become your prophet."** In the eyes of Pharaoh, Moses was a god because of his ability to make miracles happen. Yet, we all know Moses' miracles came from YHWH's power. In the eyes of many people, Jesus was a god because of his ability to make miracles happen. Yet, we all know Jesus' miracles came from YHWH's power.

The story or YHWH using His power to heal a sick woman, unbeknownst to Jesus, proves that the trinity is wrong. (Mark 5:30) **Immediately Jesus realized in himself that power had gone out of him, and he turned around in the crowd and asked: "Who touched my outer garments?"**

Since his baptism, Jesus was full of the power of YHWH (also known as holy spirit). Of course Jesus's coat did not have any power and was not full of Holy Spirit, it was Jesus who had YHWH's spirit or power within him. But when the woman touched Jesus's coat, YHWH saw her faith and healed her. The power comes from the only true God, YHWH. YHWH saw her faith and healed her by sending some power from Jesus into her. Jesus didn't even know what was going on until he felt power leave him. Perhaps he felt his energy level get smaller. Perhaps he felt tired all of a sudden. We don't know because the scriptures don't tell us. But we do know that Jesus did not control the power and did not know what happened until it was over. So we see three things not acting in unity. YHWH sees the woman's faith and sends power to heal her. Jesus didn't even know what was going on until it was all over. This proves the trinity idea, which is not in the bible, doesn't work.

Not even Jesus knows the hour of the coming of the Son of Man. (Mark 13:32) **Concerning that day or the hour nobody knows, neither the angels in heaven nor the Son, but the Father.** If they were three in one then Jesus would also know.

The Father is greater than Jesus. (John 14:28) **YOU heard that I said to YOU, I am going away and I am coming [back] to YOU. If YOU loved me, YOU would rejoice that I am going my way to the Father, because the Father is greater than I am.**

Many people are so rooted in church traditions that they can't see for themselves that the trinity is not found in the bible, that Jesus is simply YHWH's son, and that YHWH's power can be described as "holy spirit." Satan has blinded these people. They are also blinded by their own pride. Please don't be like them. Please open your eyes to a simply, biblical truth. The trinity is not in the bible. YHWH alone is God and alone is worthy of our prayers and worship.

Our next chapter is about Christmas. This is another huge stumbling block for many. Sadly, they know Jesus was not born on the 25th of December, but out of tradition and peer pressure, they follow the traditions of men at the expense of biblical truth.

11. Christmas is not Christian

Church Hypocrisy / Tradition / Lie: Jesus was born on the 25th of December. The three wise men were good guys. The star that lead the wise men to Jesus was from God.

Biblical Truth: Jesus was not born on 25 December and YHWH doesn't want you to dishonor Him by engaging in the materialism and selfishness of that unbiblical celebration. The wise men were astrologists, which the bible forbids.

Here goes a quick summary of Christmas: Jesus rebuked religious leaders who liked traditions of man more than the word of God. The bible doesn't say when Jesus was born. Jesus was not born on the 25th of December. To a true Christian, every day is a day to celebrate Jesus' sacrifice and to honor him. Santa Clause is not biblical. Worshiping saints (St. Nicolas) is not biblical and is forbidden in the bible. Being grumpy and stressed out in December is not a way to honor Jesus' life. Sad, financially stressful times are not biblical. Manger scenes are wrong because the Magi visited Jesus in a "home," not a manger (perhaps up to 2 years after Jesus' birth). No one knows the number of the Magi (why do you sing that they were 3?). Magi were astrologers (which God strictly forbids) who followed a star. Herod inquired of the magi, which resulted in Herod doing a terrible thing, killing all kids under two years old. Bad associations (even at Christmas parties) corrupt useful habits. Stay away from bad people unless doing ministry on them. Honor God and Jesus by being obedient. Worship YHWH in spirit and truth.

Christmas is a great example of a seemingly good idea gone bad. The ancient Catholic Church wanted to honor Jesus by celebrating a festival to him. The ancient church attempted Christ's Mass to redeem a favorite pagan celebration day and bring thousands of pagans into the church. They assimilated the winter solstice (the shortest day of the year with the least amount of sun light), which was a pagan celebration, with an unbiblical and erroneous celebration of Jesus's birthday. Over the years this pagan celebration has become perverted to the point that it has nothing to do with honoring Jesus.

YHWH never told us the exact day of Jesus' birthday. This is because Jews don't and never did celebrate birthdays. Furthermore, YHWH never said to celebrate birthdays, let alone Jesus' birthday. Birthday celebrations are a pagan tradition.

Jesus was not born on 25 December. The 25th of December was the winter solstice (a pagan holiday) and early Christian church leaders decided to mix the pagan date with a Christian event to redeem the date and gather more support. Who decided this? Was it God? Was it Jesus? No. It was Constantine in 336 A.D. who made this decision, not YHWH. Why should we follow a date that is not commanded by God.

Jesus was born in Bethlehem Ephrata. (Micah 5:2) **And you, O Bethlehem Ephrata, the one too little to get to be among the thousands of Judah, from you there will come out to me the one who is to become ruler in Israel, whose origin is from early times, from the days of time indefinite.**

There were two Bethlehems during biblical times. One was in Judah outside Jerusalem where Jesus was born and the other was north near Nazareth, where Jesus spend many years. How wonderful is it that the bible predicts years earlier where he would be born.

Jesus was borne when it was not yet fully winter. Winters in Bethlehem are very cold and require bringing domestic animals inside. Although Jesus was born in a manger, he was born when it was still warm enough outside for local shepherds to still be out in the fields with their flocks. (Luke 2:8) **There were also in that same country shepherds living out of doors and keeping watches in the night over their flocks. And suddenly YHWH's angel stood by them, and YHWH's glory gleamed around them, and they became very fearful.**

Astronomy is Good, Astrology is evil. Astronomy is studying stars and planets and physics (think NASA). Astrology is interpreting starts to get messages (think fortune tellers). This is like the daily horoscope. This is strictly forbidden by God. Deuteronomy 18:9 says "**When you enter the land the Lord your God is giving you, do not learn to imitate the detestable ways of the nations there. Let no one be found among you who sacrifices his son or daughter in the fire, who practices divination or sorcery, *interprets omens*, engages in witchcraft, or casts spells, or who is a medium or spirits or who consults the dead. Anyone who does these things is detestable to the Lord, and because of these detestable practices the Lord your God will drive out those nations before you."**

The Magi were led by the star. That means they were astrologists. That is a "no go" in the eyes of God. Jeremiah 10:2 says **"This is what the LORD says: "Do not act like the other nations, who try to read their future in the stars. Do not be afraid of their predictions, even though other nations are terrified by them"** (NLT).

Good power comes from Holy Spirit. Bad power comes from the devil. Magic is evil. Therefore, the Magi (same word) were evil.

The bible doesn't say there were 3 Magi. It just says Magi. (Matthew 2:1) **Now after Jesus was born in Bethlehem of Judea in the days of Herod the king, magi from the east arrived in Jerusalem.**

Magi visited a house, not a stable. The Hebrew word for house and stable are complete different so there can be no mistake. Mary and Joseph were in a house when the magi visited. (Matthew 2:11)_**After coming into the house they saw the Child with Mary His mother; and they fell to the ground and worshiped Him. Then, opening their treasures, they presented to Him gifts of gold, frankincense, and myrrh.** This fact alone proves the historical inaccuracy of manger scenes. Yet, millions of people still put them up every December.

The timeline of the Magi's visit is not specifically given so we must assume, based upon Herod's murderous actions, that it was within two years of Jesus birth. (Matthew 2:16) **Then Herod, seeing he had been outwitted by the astrologers, fell into a great rage, and he sent out and had all the boys in Bethlehem and in all its districts done away with, from two years of age and under, according to the time that he had carefully ascertained from the astrologers.**

Sadly this tragedy was predicted 600 years in Jeremiah 31:15: **"This is what YHWH has said, 'In Ramah a voice is being heard, lamentation and bitter weeping; Rachel weeping over her sons. She has refused to be comforted over her sons, because they are no more.'"**

Santa Clause is not biblical. There is no such thing in reality as a magic fat guy in red clothes who makes iPods in the North Pole with elves to give to family members you don't like.

Saints are not biblical. God wants us to only worship him, not silly saints and not Mary. Read Exodus 20: 3-5 or see chapter 17, 19.

The bible is full of many gems of knowledge for those who love YHWH and actually spend time studying it. Below is a perfect example.

For your information, Jesus was likely born around the first week of October. Do your own research of the timeline in the beginning of Luke and the Leviticus priestly service calendar in 1 Chronicles 24 and you will arrive at the same conclusion. Hint: Jesus was born how many months after John the Baptist? John was born 9 months after Zachariah served as High priest during his tribe's designated service time. When was that?

<u>11 Reasons I don't celebrate Christmas</u>[4]

1. Christmas is driven by commercialism.

2. Christmas is nowhere mentioned in the Bible.

3. Jesus wasn't born on or near Dec. 25.

4. The Christmas holiday is largely a recycled pagan celebration.

5. God condemns using pagan customs to worship Him.

6. Christmas is worshipping God in vain.

7. You can't put Christ back into something He was never in.

8. The Bible nowhere tells us to observe a holiday celebrating Jesus Christ's birth — but it clearly does tell us to commemorate His death.

9. Christmas obscures God's plan for mankind.

10. I'd rather celebrate the Holy Days Jesus Christ and the Apostles observed.

11. Constantine, not YHWH, declared it Jesus' birthday (This is a lie. Why observe and celebrate a lie?)

I want to spend a few seconds getting personal with you about Christmas so you can learn from my experience. Like you, I always knew that Jesus was not born on the 25th of December but because I love Jesus, I thought it was as good of a time as any other to celebrate and honor him.

Also, I didn't want to be the only "weirdo" to not celebrate Christmas. But don't worry, there are millions of true hearted Christians out there who don't celebrate Christmas. You may have to look for them. But there are millions.

When my wife and I told our families that we would not celebrate Christmas for the above explained reasons they all thought we were crazy. Our kids were the most disappointed. Even though we were doing the right thing, the first year without Christmas was hard. That was the year we threw away all our Christmas decorations and Christmas music and that year our families were the meanest to us. The second year was easier as we knew we could do it and the family got more tolerant of our integrity. And by the third year, it was absolutely pain free, drama free. So please

---

[4] http://www.ucg.org/holidays-and-holy-days/top-10-reasons-why-i-dont-celebrate-christmas/

take courage that it is possible to love YHWH and Jesus His son but to not celebrate Christmas. But expect drama and stupidity from your associates and family when you first take a stand against a tradition of man which violates biblical truth.

Let's now discuss Easter, another hypocritical church tradition which violates so many biblical truths.

12. Easter doesn't Honor YHWH

Church Hypocrisy / Tradition / Lie: Jesus was resurrected on Easter Sunday.

Biblical Truth: Jesus died at Passover, not Easter. Easter doesn't honor Jesus's sacrifice, is celebrated on the incorrect day, is pagan, and certainly not scriptural.

Easter is another good idea turned bad. The Catholic Church many centuries ago decided to incorporate celebrating the memorial of Jesus' death with a pagan harvest celebration to a goddess (again another demon pretending to be a god) whose name is a variation of the word Easter. This celebration brought in thousands of pagans who worshiped this false goddess during harvest time fertility parties. Bunny rabbits, as many know, reproduce rapidly. That is why they were adopted as a symbol of Easter's fertility and harvest celebrations. Eggs are also a symbol of new life so they were adopted into the symbols of Easter to signify the new life of Easter's fertility and harvest celebrations.

The Catholic Encyclopedia even admits that Easter is named after a false god. "The English term, according to the Ven. Bede (De temporum ratione, I, v), relates to Estre, a Teutonic goddess of the rising light of day and spring"[5].

Jesus died during Passover. You can read this for yourself in the gospels. We can see in Luke 22:7-8 that Jesus had the last supper on the day of the Passover sacrifice: **The day of the unfermented cakes now arrived, on which the Passover [victim] must be sacrificed; and he dispatched Peter and John, saying: "Go and get the Passover ready for us to eat."**

Because the Jewish day began right after sundown and ended as the sun went down, Jesus had the Passover dinner with his disciples, ordered the tradition of drinking wine and bread in remembrance of him, prayed in Gethsemane, was arrested, tortured and died all the same day. As we see in the Luke 22:7 scripture, he did this on the Passover sacrifice day. Jesus was, in fact, our Passover sacrifice, once and for all.

If you were married on Saturday the 14th of a particular month, you would not celebrate your anniversary each year during the second Saturday of that particular month. You would celebrate your anniversary on the 14th, regardless of what day of the week it was. Likewise, Jesus was sacrificed on the 14th of the month of Nissan and so true worshipers should celebrate Jesus' ransom sacrifice during the 14th of Nissan.

---

[5] Catholic Encyclopedia, New Advent, http://www.newadvent.org/cathen/05224d.htm

False religion celebrates the ransom on the wrong day. That is you and your church. You celebrate Jesus' sacrifice not on the 14th of Nissan but in accordance with directions and guidance set forth by faker catholic church leaders on the first Sunday after the third full moon after the winter solstice. It is easy to justify since all the Christendom does it. But just because so many millions do it wrongly, does that make it right? Would you celebrate your wedding anniversary on the wrong date? Would that honor your spouse?

False religion celebrates Jesus' ransom with pagan symbols and activities. Fake religion incorporates pagan celebrations with false dates, ignores biblical truth, and doesn't honor Jesus' sacrifice.

If you celebrate Easter you are a faker Christian and are outside the will of YHWH.

True Christians must worship in spirit and truth. (John 4:24)-**God is a Spirit, and those worshiping him must worship with spirit and truth."**

Like Christmas, the first year my wife and I did not celebrate Easter all our friends and family thought we were crazy or joining an occult sect. But this holiday tradition is so off from the truth and so obviously not celebrated on the right timeline (meaning not celebrated during Passover) that it was intellectually and emotionally simple to stop celebrating. Please know that there are millions of YHWH loving Christians out there who don't celebrate Easter.

YOU ARE NOT ALONE!

And more importantly, YHWH sees that you are trying to worship Him in truth. When your family and faker Christian friends all think you are crazy then you will know for sure that you are doing the right thing.

13. Suffering is not caused by YWHW

Church Hypocrisy / Tradition / Lie: Sometimes death and pain and suffering comes from God or are tests from God.

Biblical Truth: YHWH doesn't cause suffering. Suffering is a result of human sin, Satan, or chance and unforeseen circumstances.

Life is hard. No matter how rich you are or how isolated you are, you are going to experience pain.

You can't hide from suffering. We all eventually get touched by hardship. The problem is that most people don't know the source of their suffering and many faker Christians imply or even say that YHWH is the cause of this suffering.

YHWH is our father, creator. He loves people and wants the best for all of us. He wants us to know and love Him and to be obedient children. God is love. (1 John 4:8) **He that does not love has not come to know God, because God is love.**

YHWH cares for you. (1 Peter 5:6-7) **Humble yourselves, therefore, under the mighty hand of God, that he may exalt YOU in due time; while YOU throw all YOUR anxiety upon him, because he cares for YOU.**

God doesn't tempt people. Many faker Christians imply that God is testing them and tempting them to see the strength of their faith. This is bad theology and not true. Satan tempts people. People give into their own desires and sin. Sin then leads to death. Jesus' brother James reminds us that YHWH doesn't tempt people. (James 1:13-14) **When being under trial, let no one say: "I am being tried by God." For with evil things God cannot be tried nor does he himself try anyone.**

Suffering is caused by one of three things: (1) Satan (2) Human Sin, and (3) Chance or Unforeseen Circumstances

<u>Satan:</u> 1 John 5:19 reveals to us the simple truth that Satan is the ruler of the world: **The whole world is lying in the power of the wicked one.** Satan and his demons mislead people into sin and evilness. For an example of suffering caused by pure evil, think of all the thousands of people killed each week by narcotic traffickers and drug dealers as cocaine grown in Colombia is flown from Venezuela into Central America, then transported through Mexico to the hands of a despicable drug dealer who sells it to the teenage daughter of your faker Christian Sunday school teacher.

Human Sin: Sin came into the world thru one man, Adam. Romans 3:23 reminds us of the simple fact that we are all sinners: **For all have sinned and fall short of the glory of God**. Jeremiah 10:23 illustrates that men, left up to themselves, always mess things up: **I well know, O YHWH, that to earthling man his way does not belong. It does not belong to man who is walking even to direct his step.** We have to endure the consequences of sin.

Chance or Unforeseen Circumstances: Accidents happen. People find out they are allergic to bee stings when the antidote is not available. Motorcycle riders know that they take their lives into their own hands every time they turn on their bikes. A car pops a tire. Ecclesiastes 9:11-12 tells us that we are all vulnerable to chance occurrences and unforeseen anomalies: **I returned to see under the sun that the swift do not have the race, nor the mighty ones the battle, nor do the wise also have the food, nor do the understanding ones also have the riches, nor do even those having knowledge have the favor; because time and unforeseen occurrence befall them all. For man also does not know his time. Just like fishes that are being taken in an evil net, and like birds that are being taken in a trap, so the sons of men themselves are being ensnared at a calamitous time, when it falls upon them suddenly.**

My teenage daughter just talked to my wife and I recently about this very subject of suffering. She was concerned about how a loving God could allow this world to be so bad and why would He cause so much suffering. It was a very real and heart felt conversation. We explained to her that God does not cause suffering and showed her the causes of suffering. But just knowing the causes of suffering doesn't make suffering go away. But for sure, knowing the causes of suffering prevents you from blaming YHWH and drifting away from Him.

YHWH never makes people suffer. God is love.

Your suffering is either part of the devil's schemes, the consequences of your sin or the sins of others, or a result of chance and unforeseen circumstances. Please never blame YHWH for human suffering.

14. Death is Darkness / Unconsciousness

Church Hypocrisy / Tradition / Lie: When you die you go instantly to heaven to live forever. Everyone goes to heaven, except maybe Hitler or Osama Bin Laden. Some Catholics go to purgatory first where they suffer and work out penance (punishment) until they are righteous enough to get into heaven.

Biblical Truth: When you die you go to "Hades" or "Sheol" where you are powerless and conscious of nothing, awaiting resurrection and judgement.

Everyone Dies. Well, at least that used to be the case. But since we are living in the last days, there will be many of us who endure through the great tribulation and fear inspiring Day of Judgment, and who will be able to live forever. Whether you will live forever or die tomorrow, it is important to know what YHWH's plan for death entails because it can give you hope during this time of trouble and will help you recognize false religion and their false doctrines.

Death was not a part of YHWH's original plan. Death occurred when Adam was disobedient.

(Romans 5:12) **That is why, just as through one man sin entered into the world and death through sin, and thus death spread to all men because they had all sinned.**

YHWH even warned Adam that he would die if he was disobedient. (Genesis 2:16-17) **And YHWH God also laid this command upon the man: "From every tree of the garden you may eat to satisfaction. But as for the tree of the knowledge of good and bad you must not eat from it, for in the day you eat from it you will positively die."**

In order to study death you need to become familiar with two Greek words and one Hebrew word which are frequently mistranslated by faker Christian organizations as "hell."

Origin	Word	Meaning
Greek	Hades	Common Grave
Hebrew	Sheol	Common Grave
Greek	Gehenna	Total Destruction, Lake of Fire

In summary, the bible tells us that people who have died are waiting or resting in "Hades" or "Sheol." They are dead and conscious of nothing. They are then awakened (resurrected) into life or judgment. Of those resurrected to everlasting life, most will be resurrected to live in paradise earth. 144,000 specially "elected" or "anointed" people are resurrected to be in heaven so they can serve with Jesus. Sadly, those resurrected for judgment are sent to "Gehenna" for complete destruction.

Sheol and Hades describe the same thing.

Ecclesiastes 9:5 is a great place to start because it illustrates that that those who are dead are conscious of nothing at all. **For the living are conscious that they will die; but as for the dead, they are conscious of nothing at all, neither do they anymore have wages, because the remembrance of them has been forgotten.**

The dead are not able to think. (Psalm 146:4) **His spirit goes out, he goes back to his ground; In that day his thoughts do perish.** This is a good scripture for those who claim to be dead and wake up to tell grandiose stories about their experience. These people were never fully dead. They may have had no heart beat or electrical activity for a short time, both of which can be elongated with the cold, but there was enough life giving blood and oxygen for them to survive once their system restarted.

Although I don't want to ever put YHWH in a box, these people's memories of heaven and the light at the end of the tunnel are either demonically inspired, self-accrediting dreams about their preexisting false expectations, or memories made by misleading psychologists and religious leaders who ask leading questions. The bible tells us that when you die your body stops and you are no longer conscious of anything. It is blackness.

Hades or Sheol are silent. (Psalm 115:17) **The dead themselves do not praise Jah, Nor do any going down into silence.**

The good and the bad both die and go to Sheol. A great example of this is in Job when he is complaining about God's anger and says that he would rather be dead. Job was a righteous man who YHWH favored. Certainly if he assumes he is going to Sheol then it must be a place for good people as well as bad people. (Job 14:13) **"O that in Sheol you would conceal me, That you would keep me secret until your anger turns back, That you would set a time limit for me and remember me!"**

There is no work or knowledge or wisdom in Sheol. (Ecclesiastes 5:10) **All that your hand finds to do, do with your very power, for there is no work nor devising nor knowledge nor wisdom in She'ol, the place to which you are going.** This is an important scripture for Catholics to know. The Catholic Church falsely teaches that when people die, many go to purgatory, an interim location between heaven and earth where humans work out their righteousness.

First, this is an assimilation of Greek mythology and their belief in the underworld. Secondly, purgatory is not a word found in the bible nor is it a biblical truth. When you die and are in Sheol, you are conscious of nothing and therefore do not work.

When you die, your body returns to dust. (Genesis 3:19) **In the sweat of your face you will eat bread until you return to the ground, for out of it you were taken. For dust you are and to dust you will return.** Psalms 90:3 also confirms that when man dies he becomes dust: **You make mortal man return to dust..."**

The dead are dead and do not have emotions. (Ecclesiastes 9:6) **Also, their love and their hate and their jealousy have already perished, and they have no portion anymore to time indefinite in anything that has to be done under the sun.** This means that dead people do not become evil spirits who have evil opinions and harbor resentment against the living. They have no emotions. They are dead.

The dead are not able to scare you, hurt you, kill you, and haunt you. (Isaiah. 26:14) **They are dead; they will not live. Impotent in death, they will not rise up.** The dead have no power. Voodoo witch doctors who live in grass huts and modern day catholic priests with gold rings and funny hats all ignore this truth that the dead are impotent. Many cultures in Africa even spend fortunes during burial ceremonies so that their dead loved one is happy with his burial so that he is appeased and will not be angry with them and haunt them as a ghost. This is not factual. The dead are impotent. There is no reason to pray to them, be in fear of them, worry about them, say rosaries to them, and donate money on their behalf. The dead are dead.

Spiritists do not communicate with the dead but communicate with demons who are pretending to be the dead. As we read previously, Satan and his demons can transform themselves into angels of light or other things to mislead the earth[6]. Their only goal is to take people away from true worship of YHWH the almighty. Yes it is scary stuff. Yes demons can talk like your dead loved one or feared one. Yes demons have power and strength. This is why YHWH warns us not to give the devil a foot hold. This is why YHWH warns us against getting involved in spiritism.

[6] 2 Corinthians 11: 14-15

YHWH forbade spiritism. (Leviticus 19:31) **Do not turn yourselves to the spirit mediums, and do not consult professional foretellers of events, so as to become unclean by them. I am YHWH YOUR God.**

YHWH detests spiritists. (Deuteronomy 18:10-12) **There should not be found in you anyone who makes his son or his daughter pass through the fire, anyone who employs divination, a practicer of magic or anyone who looks for omens or a sorcerer, or one who binds others with a spell or anyone who consults a spirit medium or a professional foreteller of events or anyone who inquires of the dead. For everybody doing these things is something detestable to YHWH, and on account of these detestable things YHWH your God is driving them away from before you.**

Spiritism is listed as one of the evil works of the flesh which prevents people from entering the kingdom of God. (Galatians 5:19-21) **Now the works of the flesh are manifest, and they are fornication, uncleanness, loose conduct, idolatry, practice of spiritism, enmities, strife, jealousy, fits of anger, contentions, divisions, sects, envies, drunken bouts, revelries, and things like these. As to these things I am forewarning YOU, the same way as I did forewarn YOU, that those who practice such things will not inherit God's kingdom.**

Let's do a quick case study of the prophet Samuel. YHWH performed many miracles through Samuel so modern day faker Catholics and Orthodox would call him a saint. Samuel died over two thousand years ago. So trying to communicating with Samuel would be called spiritism, which YHWH forbids and detests. Praying to this dead man is called spiritism, which YHWH forbids and detests. Asking this dead man to intercede for you is called spiritism, which YHWH forbids and detests. Worshiping this dead man is called spiritism, which YHWH forbids and detests.

If you are catholic or orthodox and pray to or ask help from or worship or adore dead saints, then you are absolutely outside the will of YHWH and doing what YHWH forbids and detests. You are worse than a satanist and a voodoo witch doctor because you at least have access to and claim to believe inspired scriptures. Repent, stop trying to communicate with the dead saints, stop giving praise and worship and false credit and power to dead humans and demons. Worship the only true, living god, YHWH.

The bible is so refreshingly honest. It frequently tells good and bad stories and gives good and bad examples. We can learn just as much from bad examples as we can from good examples.

1 Samuel 28 records one of these perfect examples of what not to do. Saul is sad and misses Samuel the prophet, who has died. So Saul goes to the witch or spiritist of Endor to try to communicate with dead Samuel. When he does this he is breaking the law of YHWH. He furthermore doesn't get any advice from Samuel, because Samuel is dead. But Saul does get terrible news and a rebuke from the demon pretending to be Samuel. Why did this demon pretending to be Samuel give him bad advice and a rebuke? We don't know for sure but perhaps, and again I say perhaps, YHWH is showing us that He is all powerful and that He can easily control a meager demon like he can easily control a donkey (Numbers 22) or a human to send His message. He is YHWH and He can't be put in a box, or a cathedral or chapel or a tent or anything built by man.

The account of Saul and the witch or spiritist of Endor is insightful because the spiritist, through her communication with the demon pretending to be Samuel, learned that Saul was pretending to be someone else. (1 Samuel 28:12) **When the woman saw "Samuel" she began crying out at the top of her voice; and the woman went on to say to Saul: "Why did you trick me, when you yourself are Saul?"** This should be warning enough that there is power (evil power) in spiritism. Stay away from it. This is a command from YHWH. And it is a warning for your everlasting safety.

Let's move on.

The bible describes many people who are dead as sleeping. Mark 5:39 tells a story of Jesus raising a little girl from death. **"Why are YOU causing noisy confusion and weeping? The young child has not died, but is sleeping."**

Lazarus's death is another example where Jesus himself compares death and being in Sheol with sleeping. (John 11:11-14) **He said these things, and after this he said to them: "Lazarus our friend has gone to rest, but I am journeying there to awaken him from sleep." Therefore the disciples said to him: Lord, if he has gone to rest, he will get well." Jesus had spoken, however, about his death. But they imagined he was speaking about taking rest in sleep. At that time, therefore, Jesus said to them outspokenly: "Lazarus has died."**

Stephen dies and Luke, under inspiration of Holy Spirit, describes it in Acts 7:60 as falling asleep: **then, bending his knees, he cried out with a strong voice: "YHWH, do not charge this sin against them." And after saying this he fell asleep [in death].**

Now let's transition to Gehenna which is synonymous with destruction and or the lake of fire. Figuratively, Gehenna means total destruction. Literally, Gehenna or the

Valley of Hinnom was a deep ravine outside of Jerusalem where people tossed their trash and filth. In biblical times, the trash and filth were burning all the time. It was a great literal representation of destruction.

After the first death where people go to Sheol or Hades, those resurrected for judgment are destroyed. They are sent to the second death which is total destruction or the lake of fire. (Revelations 20:13-14) **And the sea gave up those dead in it, and death and Hades gave up those dead in them, and they were judged individually according to their deeds. And death and Hades were hurled into the lake of fire. This means the second death, the lake of fire. Furthermore, whoever was not found written in the book of life was hurled into the lake of fire.**

The ungodly will go to complete destruction. (2 Thessalonians 1: 6-9) **This takes into account that it is righteous on God's part to repay tribulation to those who make tribulation for YOU, but, to YOU who suffer tribulation, relief along with us at the revelation of the Lord Jesus from heaven with his powerful angels in a flaming fire, as he brings vengeance upon those who do not know God and those who do not obey the good news about our Lord Jesus. These very ones will undergo the judicial punishment of everlasting destruction from before the Lord and from the glory of his strength.**

Most faker Christian churches do not understand death and say that it involves cruel, everlasting fiery torment. The faker Christian church uses Luke 16:22-26 and the parable of "the rich man" and "Lazarus" to scare people into going to church. A loving God judges justly, and would never give everlasting torment as a punishment to someone who did not love Him. This scriptural parable was recorded to emphasize the importance of honoring YHWH and that having the text of the bible is enough for anyone to find YHWH.

Most faker Christian churches do not understand the timeline of dying. When you die you are dead, conscious of nothing, dust. You go to paradise after the resurrection, not the second you die. Let's take a close look at what Jesus said in Luke 23:43: **And he said to him: "Truly I tell you today, You will be with me in Paradise."** Please note that in the original scrolls there is a punctuation mark after the word "today." If there was no punctuation mark then Jesus would be saying that that day (immediately after dying) they would be in paradise. But because there is a pause after today, Jesus is saying something similar to "right now in this moment I am saying that when you are resurrected you will receive paradise." Many churches say things like "she is now looking down on us from heaven." This is not so. Your loved one is dead and in Hades or Sheol, black, conscious of nothing, dust, waiting to be resurrected.

In summary: Someone dies. This is the first death. They are in Sheol or Hades, asleep in death, conscious of nothing, powerless. They will wait until the resurrection where they will be judged. If they are judged worthy, they get everlasting life. If they are judged unworthy of everlasting life they will go to Gehenna, the lake of fire, for total destruction. This is the second death. The dead are not tormented by fire. They are not in purgatory working out their salvation and praying to dead saints. They are not in heaven floating on clouds with angelic fat kids with wings and bows and arrows.

Let's take a greater look what the bible says about this resurrection and judgement.

15. Everyone is Resurrected for Individual Judgment

Church Hypocrisy / Tradition / Lie: When you die you go instantly to heaven to live forever. Everyone goes to heaven, except maybe Hitler or Osama Bin Laden. Some Catholics go to purgatory first where they suffer and work out penance (punishment) until they are righteous enough to get into heaven.

Biblical Truth: Everyone is individually judged face to face based upon their works and receives a just verdict of everlasting life or destruction.

Many false religions say that when you die you immediately will live forever in heaven or in paradise. This is wrong. The bible clearly states that we will all be raised up for a resurrection, a resurrection into everlasting life or into judgment and destruction. That is why it is important to honor YHWH with all your heart, mind, soul, strength and to be obedient.

The bible clearly teaches that everyone dead (both the righteous and unrighteous) will be resurrected so that Jesus can render a face to face judgment to them based upon the deeds of their life. Jesus will separate the sheep from the goats. The sheep will go to everlasting life and the goats will go to everlasting destruction.

Thankfully, it is not our responsibility to judge others. Jesus sees their hearts, knows extenuating circumstances, and will render a fair, just verdict. Even though it is not our job to judge, we can easily recognize and avoid sin and those whose ways do not honor YHWH.

Everyone dead will be resurrected

There will be a resurrection of the righteous and unrighteous. (Acts 24:15) **And I have hope toward God, which hope these [men] themselves also entertain, that there is going to be a resurrection of both the righteous and the unrighteous.**

Both the righteous and wicked will be judged. (Ecclesiastes 3:17) **So I said in my heart: "The true God will judge both the righteous and the wicked, for there is a time for every activity and every action."**

Everyone will be resurrected. (Isaiah 26:19) **"Your dead ones will live. A corpse of mine—they will rise up. Awake and cry out joyfully, YOU residents in the dust! For your dew is as the dew of mallows and the earth itself will let even those impotent in death drop [in birth].**

Judgment will be face to face and individual.

Everyone will be judged individually. (Deuteronomy 7: 9-11) **You well know that YHWH your God is the true God, the faithful God, keeping his covenant and loyal love to a thousand generations of those who love him and keep his commandments. But those who hate him he will repay to their face with destruction. He will not be slow to deal with those who hate him; he will repay them to their face.**

Therefore, take care to keep the commandments and the regulations and the judicial decisions that I am commanding you today, by observing them.

Men will be judged individually for their deeds. (Revelation 20:13) **And the sea gave up those dead in it, and death and Ha′des gave up those dead in them, and they were judged individually according to their deeds.**

Judgment will be based upon deeds and conduct.

We will be repaid according to our conduct. (2 Corinthians 5:10) **For we must all appear before the judgment seat of the Christ, so that each one may be repaid according to the things he has practiced while in the body, whether good or bad.**

YHWH may destroy you because of what you say or do on earth. (Ecclesiastes 5:6) **Do not allow your mouth to cause you to sin, and do not say before the angel that it was a mistake. Why make the true God indignant over what you say so that he has to destroy the work of your hands?**

You will be judged according to your deeds. (Revelation 20:12) **And I saw the dead, the great and the small, standing before the throne, and scrolls were opened. But another scroll was opened; it is the scroll of life. The dead were judged out of those things written in the scrolls according to their deeds.**

Jesus Judges

Exercise faith in Jesus. (John 11:25) **Jesus said to her: "I am the resurrection and the life. He that exercises faith in me, even though he dies, will come to life."** It is essential to point out that Jesus's expression is not "having faith in me" but is "exercising faith in me." Exercising implies work and a deliberate effort.

Jesus has been given the authority to do the judging. (John 5:25-29) **Most truly I say to YOU, The hour is coming, and it is now, when the dead will hear the voice of the Son of God and those who have given heed will live. For just as the Father has life in himself, so he has granted also to the Son to have life in himself. And he has given him authority to do judging, because Son of man he is. Do not marvel at this, because the hour is coming in which all those in the memorial**

tombs will hear his voice and come out, those who did good things to a resurrection of life, those who practiced vile things to a resurrection of judgment.

YHWH has the power to resurrect but Jesus does the judging. (John 5: 21-22) **For just as the Father raises the dead up and makes them alive, so the Son also makes alive whomever he wants to. For the Father judges no one at all, but he has entrusted all the judging to the Son.**

Jesus will judge. (Acts 10:42) **Also, he ordered us to preach to the people and to give a thorough witness that this is the one decreed by God to be judge of the living and the dead.**

Jesus is the one appointed to judge. (Acts 17:31) **Because he has set a day on which he purposes to judge the inhabited earth in righteousness by a man whom he has appointed, and he has provided a guarantee to all men by resurrecting him from the dead.**

Jesus will judge the living and the dead. (2 Timothy 4:1-2) **I solemnly charge you before God and Christ Jesus, who is destined to judge the living and the dead, and by his manifestation and his kingdom, preach the word, be at it urgently in favorable season, in troublesome season, reprove, reprimand, exhort, with all long-suffering and [art of] teaching.**

There are two verdicts: Everlasting life or Destruction

All those judged will go to everlasting life or destruction. (Matthew 25:31-33,46) **When the Son of man arrives in his glory, and all the angels with him, then he will sit down on his glorious throne. And all the nations will be gathered before him, and he will separate people one from another, just as a shepherd separates the sheep from the goats. And he will put the sheep on his right hand, but the goats on his left.** (46) **And these will depart into everlasting cutting-off, but the righteous ones into everlasting life.**

Those YHWH gave Jesus will have everlasting life. (John 6:39-40) **This is the will of him that sent me, that I should lose nothing out of all that he has given me but that I should resurrect it at the last day. For this is the will of my Father, that everyone that beholds the Son and exercises faith in him should have everlasting life, and I will resurrect him at the last day.**

Jesus will fairly judge those destined for destruction. (John 5:28-29) **Do not marvel at this, because the hour is coming in which all those in the memorial tombs will**

hear his voice and come out, those who did good things to a resurrection of life, those who practiced vile things to a resurrection of judgment.

The road to everlasting life is very narrow. So if you are a faker Christian then don't take anything for granted. (Matthew 7:13) **Go in through the narrow gate; because broad and spacious is the road leading off into destruction, and many are the ones going in through it; whereas narrow is the gate and cramped the road leading off into life, and few are the ones finding it.**

Faker Christians will not enter the Kingdom. (Matthew 7:21-23) **Not everyone saying to me, 'Lord, Lord,' will enter into the kingdom of the heavens, but the one doing the will of my Father who is in the heavens will. Many will say to me in that day, 'Lord, Lord, did we not prophesy in your name, and expel demons in your name, and perform many powerful works in your name?' And yet then I will confess to them: I never knew YOU! Get away from me, YOU workers of lawlessness".**

Many people say they do not believe in God. They will. This is because everyone will be resurrected for judgment. Some ask why would a loving God resurrect someone only to send them off to destruction?

The answer is simple. YHWH deserved honor and glory and respect and worship and praise. And He will get it from everyone. He gets it now from those who love him and will continue to love Him forever. And those who could care less about Him now will certainly give Him respect when they see His remarkable grandeur and glory as they realize that they choose poorly. Sadly, many will regret that they followed false traditions of the church instead of doing what YHWH says through the bible.

16. Your Soul can be Destroyed

Church Hypocrisy / Tradition / Lie: Your soul is immortal and will absolutely live forever. When you die, your soul goes hell where it suffers forever, or it goes to "purgatory" where it is punished and purified, and then lives forever in heaven with God and a lot of fat, baby-like angels.

Biblical Truth: A soul is life, a living being. It belongs to YHWH. Only YHWH can destroy your soul. There is no such thing as purgatory.

There are many incorrect ideas about the "soul" circulating within the faker Christian church. The laws of logic tell us that they all could be wrong, but they certainly cannot all be right. So let's look at what we know and can prove from the bible.

The bible clearly teaches that:

1. A soul is a living creature or a living being
2. Animals and humans are souls (living creatures)
3. Our souls (lives) belong to YHWH
4. Only YHWH can kill our soul

That is it. This is what we can know for sure. The bible doesn't teach about dying and going to purgatory where we suffer for as long as we need to in order to be purified of our sins. This is a false tradition of the Catholic church.

Let's look at the above four concepts in greater detail…

1. A soul is a living creature or a living being

"Soul" is translated from the Hebrew word "Nephes" and the Greek word "psyche." "Nephes" is found in the bible 754 times and Psykhe occurs 102 times. Nephes means breath as in "has breath" or "is a breathing creature." Psykhe is familiar to most of us because of words like psychology and is related to mind. Soul is having a mind and the breath of life, a living creature.

Genesis 2:7 is a good scripture to study because it clearly uses the word Nephes as a living creature, person, being or soul. Let's look at it from several translations. Please note that Nephes has been translated into "living person," or "living creature," or "living being," or living soul".

New Living Translation: Then the LORD God formed the man from the dust of the ground. He breathed the breath of life into the man's nostrils, and the man became a living person.

English Standard Version: Then the LORD God formed the man of dust from the ground and breathed into his nostrils the breath of life, and the man became a living creature.

Young's Literal Translation: And YHWH God formeth the man -- dust from the ground, and breatheth into his nostrils breath of life, and the man becometh a living creature.

New American Standard Bible: Then the LORD God formed man of dust from the ground, and breathed into his nostrils the breath of life; and man became a living being.

Holman Christian Standard Bible: Then the LORD God formed the man out of the dust from the ground and breathed the breath of life into his nostrils, and the man became a living being.

King James Bible: And the LORD God formed man *of* the dust of the ground, and breathed into his nostrils the breath of life; and man became a living soul.

American Standard Version: And YHWH God formed man of the dust of the ground, and breathed into his nostrils the breath of life; and man became a living soul.

World English Bible: Yahweh God formed man from the dust of the ground, and breathed into his nostrils the breath of life; and man became a living soul.

There are hundreds of examples of "soul" in the bible so if you need to do additional research then please do so.

2. Animals and humans are souls (living creatures)

Adam became a living creature. (1 Cor. 15:45) **It is even so written: 'The first man Adam became a living soul.' The last Adam became a life-giving spirit.** Please note that Adam, the first man, "became" a soul. It doesn't say that he had a soul. He became a soul. Becoming a soul means becoming a living creature.

People are (souls) living creatures. (1 Pet. 3:20) **In Noah's days, a few people, that is, eight souls, were carried safely through the water.**

Animals also are (souls) living creatures. We see this in many scriptures. Below you can read a few examples:

Animals are (souls) living creatures. (Genesis 1:20) **God went on to say: 'Let the waters swarm forth a swarm of living souls.'** Obviously if YHWH calls fish souls then the meaning of the word soul must be living creature.

The same word for soul is used for man and animals. (Leviticus 24:17-18) **In case a man strikes any soul of mankind fatally, he should be put to death without fail. And the fatal striker of the soul of a domestic animal should make compensation for it, soul for soul.**

3. Our souls (lives) belong to YHWH

Living creatures (souls) belong to YHWH. And if they sin, they die. (Ezek. 18:4) **Look! All the souls—to me they belong. As the soul of the father so likewise the soul of the son—to me they belong. The soul that is sinning—it itself will die.**

A (soul) living creature can be killed. (Matthew 10:39) **Whoever finds his soul will lose it, and whoever loses his soul for my sake will find it.** We are encourages to die to ourselves and to live for YHWH.

If we live for YHWH in this world then we will inherit the kingdom. If we only live for ourselves in this world then we certainly will not have the opportunity to inherit the kingdom of God. In other words, if we are bad in this world we will be destroyed during the judgement.

4. Only YHWH can kill our soul

Only YHWH can kill our soul. (Matthew 10:28) **And do not become fearful of those who kill the body but cannot kill the soul; but rather be in fear of him that can destroy both soul and body in Gehenna.** This is a very important scripture because it tells us that man can kill our body but man can't kill our souls. So when our bodies die, our souls do not die. Our soul can only be destroyed by YWHW in Gehenna.

What happens to our soul during the time between when we die and when we are resurrected to everlasting life? Great question? The bible doesn't tell us exactly how that works, but we know for sure that when we die, we rest and wait in unconsciousness in Hades or Sheol until the judgement. After judgement, we receive either destruction in Gehenna or everlasting life. If our souls is destroyed in Gehenna then it is obviously mortal and destroyable. This proves that the Catholic church's tradition of the "immortal soul" is not biblical. But if our souls are not destroyed in Gehenna, then we can assume that our souls (our lives as living creatures) will keep on living during everlasting life. In this sense, our souls live forever.

How the resurrection process specifically works is unknown. Are we resurrected young or old or in new bodies or born again as babies? I don't even want to speculate about how we are resurrected. I don't want to put YHWH in a box or to limit His abilities. YHWH is in charge of that amazing process. But we can trust in YHWH who made this system and have confidences that the joys of the resurrection are worth any sacrifice me make in this current world to remain obedient and loyal to YHWH.

Let's summarize what we learned about the soul: A soul is a living creature or a living being. Animals and humans are souls (living creatures). Our souls (lives) belong to YHWH. Only YHWH can kill our soul.

17. Saints, Idols, Images, Crosses & Statues Dishonor YHWH

Church Hypocrisy / Tradition / Lie: It is OK to pray to saints or to their statues or necklaces. It is OK to have idols in your church or house. It is OK to have a cross in your house or church or around your neck and to pray to it.

Biblical Truth: Saints are dead and powerless. Statues and jewelry and images are powerless. Pray to and worship YHWH and YHWH alone.

YHWH made the world in six days and rested on the seventh (not because he needed to rest but to set a perfect example for us). He is all powerful, all knowing, and timeless. If we make a statue of an old guy with a great beard and worship it then we are limiting YHWH. YHWH can't be limited. **YHWH can't be put in a box**. That is why YHWH tells us over and over again never to make anything so as to worship it.

YHWH doesn't live in a manmade place like a house, temple, or church. (2 Samuel 7:6-7) **For I have not dwelt in a house from the day of my bringing the sons of Israel up out of Egypt to this day, but I was continually walking about in a tent and in a tabernacle. During all the time that I have walked about among all the sons of Israel, was there a word that I spoke with one of the tribes of Israel that I commanded to shepherd my people Israel, saying, 'Why did YOU people not build me a house of cedars?'**

YHWH is not contained in a building. (1 Kings 8:27) **But will God truly dwell upon the earth? Look! The heavens, yes, the heaven of the heavens, themselves cannot contain you; how much less, then, this house that I have built!**

Don't put YHWH into a box. Don't limit YHWH to a statue or idol. (Acts 17:29) **Therefore, since we are the children of God, we should not think that the Divine Being is like gold or silver or stone, like something sculptured by the art and design of humans** Although YHWH manifests himself sometimes through various means, he is an invisible spirit.

YHWH must me worshiped in truth. (John 4:24) **God is a Spirit, and those worshiping him must worship with spirit and truth.**

If YHWH can't be contained in a huge building, then he certainly can't be contained in a picture, or image, or an idol or a statue. YHWH is everywhere, all-knowing and all powerful. We do not have special access to YHWH when we are in front of a cross at the local cathedral. The cross is inaccurate and has no power. We do not have special access to YHWH when we are looking at a statue of Jesus being tortured. The statue has no power. We do not have special access to YHWH when we are holding a pendant or rosary or necklace. The pendant or rosary or necklace has no power. We do not have special access to YHWH when we pray to a statue of a dead saint or to a statue of Jesus' mother, Mary. The saints and Mary are all dead. They have no power.

YWHW tells us not to make images of things and worship them. Let's look at the commandments in Exodus 20:2-6. **I am YHWH your God, who have brought you out of the land of Egypt, out of the house of slaves. You must not have any other gods against my face. You must not make for yourself a carved image or a form like anything that is in the heavens above or that is on the earth underneath or that is in the waters under the earth. You must not bow down to them nor be induced to serve them, because I YHWH your God am a God exacting exclusive devotion, bringing punishment for the error of fathers upon sons, upon the third generation and upon the fourth generation, in the case of those who hate me; but exercising loving-kindness toward the thousandth generation in the case of those who love me and keep my commandments.**

We are supposed to worship the creator, not things created. (Romans 1:25) …**even those who exchanged the truth of God for the lie and venerated and rendered sacred service to the creation rather than the One who created, who is blessed forever. Amen.**

Keep yourself from idols. (1 John 5:21) **Little children, guard yourselves from idols.**

Images and Idols have not power and are nothing. (Isaiah 41:29) **Look! All of them are something nonexistent._ Their works are nothing. Their molten images are wind_ and unreality.**

YWHW doesn't share his glory with powerless images. (Isaiah 42:8) **I am YHWH. That is my name; and to no one else shall I give my own glory, neither my praise to graven images.**

Idols and carved images have no power and are valueless. (Habakkuk 2:18) **Of what benefit has a carved image been, when the former of it has carved it, a molten statue, and an instructor in falsehood? When the former of its form has trusted in it, to the extent of making valueless gods that are speechless?**

Idols have no power and those who make them will also become powerless in death. (Psalm 115:3-8) **but our God is in the heavens; Everything that he delighted [to do] he has done. Their idols are silver and gold, the work of the hands of earthling man. A mouth they have, but they cannot speak; Eyes they have, but they**

cannot see; Ears they have, but they cannot hear. A nose they have, but they cannot smell. Hands are theirs, but they cannot feel. Feet are theirs, but they cannot walk; They utter no sound with their throat. Those making them will become just like them, All those who are trusting in them.

Let's get practical for a moment. Jesus is awesome. We love Jesus. Jesus was a perfect example for us. Jesus is at the right hand of YHWH. The very last verse of the book of John tells us that if all the stories about Jesus were written down, the scrolls would fill the world. (John 21:25) **There are, in fact, many other things also which Jesus did, which, if ever they were written in full detail, I suppose, the world itself could not contain the scrolls written.** If Jesus was so wonderful, why do faker Christians make images and statues and necklaces of the means by which he was tortured. Satan was so happy to torture Jesus. And you aren't much better when you wear a necklace with the image of our suffering savior.

Faker Christians are recognized by cross necklaces. True Christians are recognized by love. (John 13:35) **By this all will know that YOU are my disciples, if YOU have love among yourselves.**

Imagine you had a brother who you love very much who was killed in a motorcycle accident. Would you wear a necklace of a crashed motorcycle? That is perverted. That is not how you honor your brother. Then why would you do that with YHWH's son.

Faker Christians love images of Jesus being tortured. If you love Jesus then you want to think of his wonderful works of love. You don't want to think of the day he was tortured to death. 90% of paintings in faker churches and cathedrals and art museums are of Jesus being tortured. If you love Jesus then these images make you sad.

In a huge catholic cathedral in Paris I once encountered a very creepy statue of Pope Paul VI. (A creepy statue of a creepy man. Google him.) I was surprised to see a middle aged woman kneel down in front of it and begin to pray and cry. What was she thinking? We are supposed to pray to YHWH, the living God. We are not supposed to pray to a statue of an evil and dead faker Christian Pope.

You can't go anywhere in the world without finding a catholic cathedral or faker Christian church or a prayer room which doesn't have a statue of a saint or Jesus being tortured or Mary holding Jesus. We are supposed to pray to YHWH, the living God. We are not supposed to pray to a statue of a dead person. Sadly, millions of people visit their local cathedral every day to pray to powerless statues of their patron saints or some silly variation of the famous "Virgin of Guadalupe." We are supposed to pray to YHWH, the living God. We are not supposed to pray to a statue of dead and powerless people.

YHWH will pay back image makers. (Jeremiah 51:17-18) **Every man has behaved so unreasoningly as not to know. Every metalworker will feel ashamed because of the carved image; for his molten image is a falsehood, and there is no spirit in them. They are vanity, a work of mockery. In the time of their being given attention they will perish.**

Idols are powerless and anyone who trusts in them will also become powerless in death. (Psalm 135:15-18) **The idols of the nations are silver and gold, The work of the hands of earthling man. A mouth they have, but they can speak nothing; Eyes they have, but they can see nothing; Ears they have, but they can give ear to nothing. Also there exists no spirit in their mouth. Those making them will become just like them, Everyone who is trusting in them.**

On the Day of Judgment, YHWH will destroy graven images and idols. (Micah 5:13) **And I will cut off your graven images and your pillars from the midst of you, and you will no more bow down to the work of your hands.**

YHWH wants you to use your mind to realize that the wooden thing you pray to is powerless and detestable. (Isaiah 44:14-15) **There is one whose work is to cut down cedars. He selects a certain type of tree, an oak, And he lets it grow strong among the trees of the forest. He plants a laurel tree, and the rain makes it grow. Then it becomes fuel for a man to make fires. He takes part of it to warm himself; He builds a fire and bakes bread. But he also makes a god and worships it. He makes it into a carved image, and he bows down before it.**

If you own a cross or rosary or idols you are a faker Christian. Throw them away, clean up your life, and realize that our loving father, YHWH, is not empowered or accessed through your images and idols.

If you think it is more effective to pray with a cross or rosary in your hand you are wrong. You don't need a cross or rosary to access your loving Father in heaven.

If you think it is OK to pray to a statue or to a saint or to a dead person then you are a fake Christian. You don't need a statue or a saint to access your loving Father in heaven.

Throw away your idols, statues, crosses, rosaries, clean up your life, and realize that our loving father, YHWH, requires exclusive devotion.

18. The Cross Dishonors YHWH

Church Hypocrisy / Tradition / Lie: It is OK to have a cross in your house or church or around your neck and to pray to it and to worship it.

Biblical Truth: YHWH is not pleased with your cross necklace or statue.

Jesus died for our sins by being nailed to what the original Greek text called a "stauros" (σταυρός) or a "zylon" (ξύλον). Although these words are translated into English as a single, vertical stake or beam or pole, both of these words have been falsely translated by the early church as cross.

But before we study the history and meaning of these words, let's make a quick summary of a previous chapter.

YHWH clearly tells us in Exodus 20 and Deuteronomy 5 not to make images and statues of things and worship them. Yet, the faker protestant and catholic churches love to make images of a suffering and or dead and powerless Jesus on a cross and worship it. They pray to the cross. They pray at the cross. They finish prayers by making the sign of a cross.

The instrument of Jesus death is not something to celebrate. If your son was innocent yet put to death in the electric chair or via lethal injection would you walk around with a gold electric chair or medical syringe hanging proudly around your next? Of course not!

Stop showing off who holy you are by having a shameful gold cross on your neck and start showing YHWH your heart through **"holy acts of conduct and deeds of godly devotion"** (2 Peter 3:11).

Displaying a cross or Jesus on a cross exposes Jesus to public shame. (Hebrews 6:6) …**but have fallen away, it is impossible to revive them again to repentance, because they nail the Son of God to the stake again for themselves and expose him to public shame.**

Already, through a clear biblical commandment (in the 10 Commandments) and practical reasoning (Hebrews 6:6), we see that a cross is not something in which YHWH delights. Now let's dig deeper into our already skeptical understanding of the cross by looking at the meaning of "stauros" or "zylon" using some of the most trusted dictionaries available.

Stauros is found in the bible as Strong's Concordance word number 4716. The Vines Complete Expository Dictionary says it is

> *an upright pale or stake." On such malefactors were nailed for execution. Both the noun and the verb stauroo, "to fasten to a stake or pale," are originally to be distinguished from the ecclesiastical form of a two beamed "cross." The shape of the latter had its origin in ancient Chaldea, and was used as the symbol of the god Tammuz (being in the shape of the mystic Tau, the initial of his name) in that country and in adjacent lands, including Egypt. By the middle of the 3rd cent. A.D. the churches had either departed from, or had travestied, certain doctrines of the Christian faith. In order to increase the prestige of the apostate ecclesiastical system pagans were received into the churches apart from regeneration by faith, and were permitted largely to retain their pagan signs and symbols. Hence the Tau or T, in its most frequent form, with the cross-piece lowered, was adopted to stand for the "cross" of Christ.*

What this tells us is that the original "stauros" was a wooden stake, more like a short telephone pole. The apostate church in the third century changed the meaning of the "stauros" to cross in an attempt to increase membership. By the way, I find it ironic that "Thomas Nelson," one of the largest faker Christian "den of thieves" book publishing companies in the world prints the Vines Complete Expository Dictionary which acknowledges that the "stauros" meant upright stake, not a cross.

Below are a few more trusted definitions or stauros:

The Thayer Greek Lexicon's first definition is "an upright stake, especially a pointed one (Homer, Herodotus, Thucydides, Xenophon)."[7]

NAS exhaustive Concordance defines stauros as "an upright stake."[8]

The Strong's Exhaustive Concordance Definition stauros as "from the base of histemi; a stake or post (as set upright), i.e. (specially), a pole or cross"[9]

Stauroó (Strongs word 4717) is the verb form of Stauros. Thayer Greek Lexicon defines it as (1) "to stake, drive down stakes" or (2) to fortify with driven stakes, to

[7] http://biblehub.com/greek/4716.htm (Thayer's)
[8] http://biblehub.com/greek/4716.htm (NAS Exhaustive)
[9] http://biblehub.com/greek/4716.htm (Strong's Exhaustive)

palisade."[10] It is interesting to see that the verb for Stauroó means to drive in stakes… like you were making a fence, not make crosses or cross beams.

Vines defines Xylon (Strong's word 3586) as "wood, a piece of wood, anything made of wood" (see STAFF, STOCKS), is used, with the rendering "tree," (a) in Luke 23:31, where "the green tree" refers either to Christ, figuratively of all His living power and excellency, or to the life of the Jewish people while still inhabiting their land, in contrast to "the dry," a figure fulfilled in the horrors of the Roman massacre and devastation in A.D. 70 (cp. the Lord's parable in Luke 13:6-9; see Ezek. 20:47, and cp. Ezek. 21:3); (b) of "the cross," the tree being the stauros, the upright pale or stake to which Romans nailed those who were thus to be executed, Acts 5:30; 10:39; 13:29; Gal. 3:13; 1 Pet. 2:24".[11]

Strong's Exhausted Concordance defines Xylon as "from another form of the base of xestes; timber (as fuel or material); by implication, a stick, club or tree or other wooden article or substance -- staff, stocks, tree, wood."

Now is it easier to see that when the bible writers use the word stauros or xylon they are referring to the completely upright wooden stake upon which Jesus died for our sins.

Secular historians even agree that 1st century romans killed people with a single vertical torture stake, not a cross.

The sign which Pilate wrote above Jesus may have made his vertical torture stake look from a distance like a T or a t. However, this sign was not a cross beam upon which Jesus body and weight hung. It was merely a sign. (John 19:19-22) **Pilate wrote a title also and put it on the torture stake. It was written: "Jesus the Nazarene′ the King of the Jews." Therefore many of the Jews read this title, because the place where Jesus was impaled was near the city; and it was written in Hebrew, in Latin, in Greek. However, the chief priests of the Jews began to say to Pilate: "Do not write 'The King of the Jews,' but that he said, 'I am King of the Jews.'" Pilate answered: "What I have written I have written."**

It is sad to see that the truth about our savior was hidden by the Catholic Church in the first centuries of after his death. This wasn't too hard since the people were not allowed to have a copy of the bible to read the truth for themselves.

Sadly, the faker church has had almost 2000 years to cover up the truth that Jesus was killed on a vertical, singular piece of wood. For all of you who see the hypocrisy

---

[10] http://biblehub.com/greek/4717.htm (Thayer's)

[11] Vines Complete Expository Dictionary, Thomas Nelson, Nashville, 1996, Page 642

and lies of the church this cover up is easy to understand. For those of you who grew up with crosses and painting of the cross all over your houses, churches, and museums, it is harder to believe this truth. Please do your own research to see for yourself that the cross was a pagan symbol adopted by a false church.

Please stop worshiping a cross, stop praying to a cross and stop wearing a cross. Please clean up your life, your wardrobe, your house and throw away every cross you have. Please know that history and the original texts of the bible show that Jesus died on a singular, vertical piece of wood. This was a sad and painful time for our savior and we should honor YHWH by not having an inaccurate symbol of how His son died around our necks, in our homes, or at the place of our worship.

19. Mary Worship Dishonors YHWH

Church Hypocrisy / Tradition / Lie: Pray to and worship and adore Mary. Mary can help you because she is the most important person in Heaven.

Biblical Truth: Mary is dead (resting) and is powerless. Pray to and worship YHWH and YHWH alone.

Mary was a wonderful woman who had such a pure heart that she was chosen by YHWH for the amazing privilege and responsibility of being the mother of Jesus, YWHW's son. Yet, Mary is the source of so many theological mistakes.

YHWH says to worship him alone. (Exodus 20: 4-5) **You must not make for yourself a carved image or a form like anything that is in the heavens above or that is on the earth underneath or that is in the waters under the earth. You must not bow down to them nor be induced to serve them, because I YHWH your God am a God exacting exclusive devotion.**

We should not worship dead people or dead saints. We are not supposed to worship Jesus. We are not supposed to worship Mary. We are supposed to worship God alone.

YHWH shares his glory with no one. Not even Mary. (Isaiah 42:8) **I am YHWH. That is my name; and to no one else shall I give my own glory, neither my praise to graven images.**

YHWH doesn't share his glory with dead saints, and he won't share his glory with Mary. If you worship or glorify Mary then you make YHWH mad.

Besides the virgin birth, which was a miracle from YHWH, not Mary, the bible never records a single miracle of Mary.

Mary had sexual intercourse and is no longer a virgin. The bible clearly states that Joseph had intercourse with his wife after Jesus was born. (Matthew 1:25) **But he had no intercourse with her until she gave birth to a son; and he called his name Jesus.**

The Greek goddess Artemis from Ephesus was known for being an eternal virgin. This pagan concept of eternal virginity was assimilated by Catholics towards Jesus' mother.

Mary had other children. The bible clearly states that Jesus had siblings. (Matthew 12:46) **While he was yet speaking to the crowds, look! His mother and brothers took up a position outside seeking to speak to him.**

Read Matthew 13:55 to get the names of some of Jesus's brothers. **"Is this not the carpenter's son? Is not his mother called Mary, and his brothers James and Joseph and Simon and Judas?"**

Do some research on your own to see that the writer of the books James and Jude were Jesus' brothers.

Mary died almost 2000 years ago. As we studied in chapter 14, the dead are powerless and conscious of nothing. Therefore, Mary has no power and we should not worship her, pray to her, or give glory to her.

Praying to Mary is outside the will of YHWH. Venerating Mary is outside the will of YHWH. Glorifying Mary is outside the will of YHWH. Making statues of Mary to worship is outside the will of YHWH.

The catholic churches' immoral and unbiblical adoration of Mary alone is sufficient for me to say with a clean conscious that all Catholics are fakers. Shame on you if you pray to Mary rather than to YHWH. Satan has won. He has fooled you into worshiping someone else, besides YHWH. Shame on you if you go to a cathedral and pray and worship before a statue of a dead and powerless woman. Did you forget about the ten commandments where it says to only worship God and to not make idols? Where is your sense of reasoning? (Matthew 15:9) **It is in vain that they keep worshipping me, for they teach commands of men as doctrines**.

Sadly, so many Catholics pray to Mary. Praying to Mary is wrong. The bible tells us to only pray to YHWH. Sadly, many Protestants also pray incorrectly… when they pray to Jesus. Praying to Jesus is also wrong. Let us now study prayer.

20. Pray only to YHWH

Church Hypocrisy / Tradition / Lie: It is OK to pray to Jesus or to saints or to Mary or to dead popes.

Biblical Truth: Pray only to YHWH, but in the name of Jesus.

In this chapter we are going to discuss (1) location of prayer and (2) to whom you must direct your prayer.

Location of prayer is almost unimportant. Please don't think that to have your prayers heard you need to be in a church or in front of a statue or image. The power to hear and answer prayer comes from YHWH, the hearer of prayers, and not from the cathedral or statue of a dead Saint or Jesus's mother.

Jesus tells us to pray in a hidden place. (Matthew 6:5) **"Also, when YOU pray, YOU must not be as the hypocrites; because they like to pray standing in the synagogues and on the corners of the broad ways to be visible to men."**

A prayer made in a cathedral is actually less likely of being answered than a prayer made in your car. If you are in an old, huge, finely decorated Cathedral (think of Notre Dame Cathedral, Paris or St. Paul's Cathedral, Rome) then you are surrounded by statues and images and inside a place where false doctrine and lies have been preached by Catholic Priests for hundreds of years, misleading thousands of thousands of people away from the truth and onto the path that leads to death and judgment. But if your heart is in the right place, then YHWH will hear your prayer despite being in such a blatantly evil place. If you are praying in your car, then perhaps no one knows what you are doing and in fact you are in a hidden place or private room. This is more in line with what Jesus directed us to do. But don't forget, YHWH sees the heart. So pray from the heart.

Prayer goes to YHWH and to YHWH alone. (Philippians 4:6) **Do not be anxious over anything, but in everything by prayer and supplication along with thanksgiving let YOUR petitions be made known to God.**

YHWH is called the hearer of prayers. (Psalm 65:2) **O Hearer of prayer, even to you people of all flesh will come.**

Prayer does not go to false gods or to anyone else. Yes there are bad examples in the bible of people doing silly things to win the approval of false gods. But we know that these false gods have no power. A great example of praying and yelling out to false gods who have no power is when Elisha challenges the prophets of fake god Baal to see if fake god Baal will send down fire from the sky to consume a burn offering. (1 Kings 18:26) **So they took the young bull that he gave them. Then they dressed it, and they kept calling upon the name of Baal from morning till noon, saying: "O Baal, answer us!" But there was no voice, and there was no one answering.**

All of the heroes of the faith prayed to YHWH. Abraham prayed to YWHW. Moses prayed to YHWH. Joshua prayed to YWHW. Daniel prayed to YHWHW. Paul prayed to YWHW. I hope you get the pattern.

Not one person in the entire bible prayed to the messiah. And so we should not pray to Jesus, either.

Yet twice in the Bible we see people talking to Jesus after he ascended and was at the right hand of the Father. The first is when Stephen was stoned for telling the truth to the faker religious leaders of his time. (Acts 7: 55) **But he, being full of holy spirit, gazed into heaven and caught sight of God's glory and of Jesus standing at God's right hand.** Please note that Jesus is not in place of God. Jesus is subordinate to YHWH and is at YHWH's right hand. Stephen is not in prayer. He had a vision of the thrown of YHWH. In verses 59 and 60 Stephen speaks to Jesus and YHWH: **As they were stoning Stephen, he made this appeal: "Lord Jesus, receive my spirit." Then, kneeling down, he cried out with a strong voice: "YHWH, do not charge this sin against them." And after saying this, he fell asleep in death.** This is a remarkable story of the first martyr, not a model for how we should pray.

The second time someone speaks directly with Jesus is when John, after receiving the "revelation," tells Jesus to come soon. Revelations 22:20 **"He that bears witness of these things says, 'Yes; I am coming quickly." "Amen! Come, Lord Jesus."** In this scripture Jesus is talking to John and so John asks Jesus to come back to earth and to bring in YHWH's Kingdom. This is not the model for prayer with YHWH. This is a conversation between a blessed prophet and Jesus. Believe me, you are not a prophet and are not John's replacement for modern times.

Jesus prayed all the time. There are many examples in the bible when Jesus went off to pray. Matthew 14:23 is one example, of many, when Jesus went someplace by himself to pray. Jesus also had some heartfelt prayer in Gethsemane. (Matthew 26:36-39) **Then Jesus came with them to the spot called Gethsemane, and he said to the disciples: "Sit down here while I go over there and pray." And taking along Peter and the two sons of Zebedee, he started to be grieved and to be sorely troubled. Then he said to them: "My soul is deeply grieved, even to death. Stay here and keep on the watch with me." And going a little way forward, he**

fell upon his face, praying and saying: "My Father, if it is possible, let this cup pass away from me. Yet, not as I will, but as you will."

Jesus prayed to his father, not to himself. Jesus's longest recorded prayer in John 17 is directed to YHWH. (John 17:1) **Jesus spoke these things, and, raising his eyes to heaven, he said: "Father, the hour has come; glorify your son, that your son may glorify you.**

Jesus prayed to his father, not to himself. Jesus' model prayer teaches us to pray to YHWH. (Matthew 6:9-10) **YOU must pray, then, this way: 'Our Father in the heavens, let your name be sanctified._ Let your kingdom come. Let your will take place, as in heaven, also upon earth. Jesus showed us that we should pray to YHWH.**

When we are thankful we should pray to YHWH and give thanks in the name of Jesus. (Ephesians 5:20) **always giving thanks to our God and Father for everything in the name of our Lord Jesus Christ.**

God is the giver of gifts, but we should ask for things in the name of Jesus. (John 16:23) **And in that day YOU will ask me no question at all. Most truly I say to YOU, If YOU ask the Father for anything he will give it to YOU in my name".**

The name of Jesus is powerful. Jesus is powerful. But all of the power of Jesus' name and all the power that Jesus has is from YHWH. By referencing Jesus' name at the end of our prayers we are implying "I am in a right standing before you YHWH and am able to offer up this pray of supplication or thanksgiving only because of the access given to me by the ransom of Jesus." It is an admittance of humility, of the need for Jesus' sacrifice, and an acknowledgement that without Jesus' sacrifice we would never be able to have a right standing before YHWH, our grand creator.

If you pray to Jesus then you are wrong and outside the will of YWHW. Faker Christians all over the world pray to Jesus. Yes, we are to give thanks and ask for things in Jesus' name. But YHWH is the hearer of prayers. He is the giver of power and blessings.

If you pray to Mary, you are wrong and outside the will of YWHW. Mary was a wonderfully blessed woman but she has been dead now for almost 2000 years. She has no power. She is resting in Hades and will be resurrected when YHWH calls all of those who also have died.

If you pray to Saints, you are wrong and outside the will of YWHW.

I want to tell a sad personal story. My Catholic father recently died and out of respect for the rest of my family we decided to attend the funeral, knowing it was going to be a hypocritical church tradition, not a reflection of biblical truth. During the service, the Catholic priest asked us to all extend our arms out towards the casket and said "please join me in begging the saints to fling open the gates of heaven and welcome in our dear brother." In one sentence, this priest made so many theological errors. I wonder if he had ever read the bible. Certainly, he was ignoring it. Why would the priest beg the saints to help my father get into heaven? The saints are dead and powerless and also awaiting the resurrection. We are supposed to pray to YHWH and only to YHWH.

If you pray to inanimate things (images or statues or the cross) then you are wrong and outside the will of YWHW. Prayer need to be directed to YHWH who is not confined to a building or an image or a statue.

In an attempt to add respect and power to the things of the church, the church created the tradition of praying only in the church and praying to inanimate things. This is silly and unbiblical. The church loves to pervert biblical truth to better serve itself. Another great example of serving itself is demanding celibacy from its workers. Let us now study how celibacy amongst clergy, monks, and nuns is unbiblical and dishonors YHWH.

21. Celibacy in Clergy, Monks and Nuns Dishonors YHWH

Church Hypocrisy / Tradition / Lie: It is OK to not have children. If you love God and want to serve Him full time it is best if you become a monk or nun or priest and dedicate your life to celibacy.

Biblical Truth: Get married to someone who loves YHWH and raise a lot of Christian children together. Don't become a priest or nun. Be fruitful and multiply.

YHWH made man and woman and told them to be fruitful and multiply. (Genesis 1:27-31) **And God proceeded to create the man in his image, in God's image he created him; male and female he created them. Further, God blessed them and God said to them: "Be fruitful and become many and fill the earth and subdue it...**

Please note that YHWH made the family before he made the church and its organization.

YHWH loves marriage but he wants you to marry someone who loves YHWH as much as you do. The rule with Christian marriage is that you are only supposed to marry another Christian. (2 Corinthians 6:14) **Do not become unevenly yoked with unbelievers. For what fellowship do righteousness and lawlessness have?**

Priests of YHWH had children. Prophets of YHWH had children.

Nowhere in the bible does it say that if you love YHWH you must become celibate.

The bible does say that Satan and his demons will mislead the faker Christian church (in this case the catholic church) in the final times to make celibacy part of their doctrine. (1Timothy 4:1-3) **However, the inspired utterance says definitely that in later periods of time some will fall away from the faith, paying attention to misleading inspired utterances and teachings of demons, by the hypocrisy of men who speak lies, marked in their conscience as with a branding iron; forbidding to marry, commanding to abstain from foods which God created to be partaken of with thanksgiving by those who have faith and accurately know the truth.**

This scripture is a prophecy of "later periods of time," which is now. This prophecy says that the apostate church will have "misleading inspired utterances and teachings of demons." We see that these apostate Christian fakers are hypocrites and liars who have no consciences. They incorrectly forbid marrying.

The Catholic Church violates biblical commands and mandates that if you love YHWH and want to serve Him, you must be celibate. Men become celibate priests. Women become celibate nuns. This is a ploy by Satan to ensure that people who love YHWH do not marry and reproduce and make godly offspring who also love and serve YHWH in the future. It is obvious that Satan is using the false teachings of the Catholic Church to kill off anyone that is predisposed to love and serve YHWH. This fact is black and white in the bible.

The Catholic Church is outside the will of YHWH. No wonder there are so many sex scandals associated with the Catholic Church. Sadly, about 90% of all priest and nuns are either sexually active, have violated their vow of celibacy, or enjoy porn. Wake up people and leave the Catholic Church. How many of your sons and daughters need to be raped by sexually perverted men who teach false doctrine (which was predicted 2000 years ago in Paul's warning to Timothy) before you get out?

Please love the truth. Don't love the traditions of men over the commandments of God. (Mathew 15:3) **In reply he said to them: "Why is it YOU also overstep the commandment of God because of YOUR tradition?**

Leave false religion today!

Sadly enough, if you look at the last part of 1 Timothy 4:3 you will notice that this demonically inspired teachings will also forbid eating foods which God created to be partaken of with thanksgiving. This is exemplified through the Catholic church's policy of not eating meat on Fridays. All around the world Catholics eat only fish on Friday. Ok…back to our subject.

Yes, the bible mentions singleness. But this is for someone who has a special calling which allowed that person to focus on serving YHWH. Joshua son of Nun never married and was able to serve YHWH with all this strength. Paul was able to constantly serve YHWH as an apostle and overseer. These men had special missions which benefited from complete devotion to YHWH.

If you think you have a calling to become a celibate priest or nun then you are wrong. You do not have a calling from YHWH but you ate too much pizza the night before and your mind is all over the place. Working for the Catholic Church is outside the will of YHWH.

If you think you have a calling to stay single to "make more money" or "work on yourself" or to "have more time for help at your faker Christian church" then you are wrong.

If you think you are called to be single, then it better be so that you can do something amazingly hard in service to YHWH. Someone with a calling from YHWH to be single is someone YHWH will use and pour out like a drink offering in His service. (2 Timothy 4:6-7) **For I am already being poured out like a drink offering, and the due time for my releasing is imminent. I have fought the fine fight, I have run the course to the finish, I have observed the faith.**

People with the gift of singleness learn a foreign language and become missionaries. They become elders in the church and work 24 hours a day for YHWH.

Likely you don't have the gift of singleness, but you will need to be patient. Finding a Christian man is so hard these days. Sadly, too many men contribute to the $57 billion pornography industry[12] or play video games 20 hours a week[13] like children. These men don't know the first thing about the bible or being a Godly man. Finding a godly man is going to be hard. Don't settle and marry a loser. You will be so much happier as a lonely single than as someone who is yoked together with a faker Christian or non-Christian.

Celibate priest and nuns and monks, no matter which denomination, are outside the will of YHWH. Leave false religion, get married to someone who loves YHWH, and raise godly children.

---

[12] https://wsr.byu.edu/pornographystats

[13] http://www.addictions.com/video-games/alarming-video-game-addiction-statistics/

22. How "True Religion" Should be Organized

Church Hypocrisy / Tradition / Lie: True religion includes a well-paid hierarchy of priests and ministers and bishops who all learned the truth during seminary. The higher your rank in the church, the more God loves you and the more likely it is that your prayers are heard. The true religion is led by the Pope, who is perfect and speaks for God. True religion is powerful in the world and is a strong economic and political power.

Biblical Truth: The Kingdom of God is not a part of THIS world. God gave us guidelines for organizing true religion until His kingdom comes. If your organization doesn't look like what the bible describes as true religion then you are not a part of true religion. Leave that denomination as soon as possible.

YHWH is love. Serving YHWH is about love. YHWH's organization must be about love. The "true religion," as defined by the bible, must be about love. It is not about power. It is not about being a celebrity. It is not about kissing the ring. It is not about you or making you feel good. It is about YHWH and putting Him first.

General principles about True Religion

If you want to be great you need to serve. (Mark 9:35) **So he sat down and called the twelve and said to them: "If anyone wants to be first, he must be last of all and minister of all."**

Jesus tells us that the 1st will be last. (Matthew 19:30) **But many that are first will be last and the last first.**

YHWH's servants must be humble. (1 Peter 5:6) **Humble yourselves, therefore, under the mighty hand of God, that he may exalt YOU in due time.**

Leaders in Satan's world love power. But Jesus came to serve. (Luke 22:25-27) **But he said to them: "The kings of the nations lord it over them, and those having authority over them are called Benefactors. YOU, though, are not to be that way. But let him that is the greatest among YOU become as the youngest, and the one acting as chief as the one ministering. For which one is greater, the one reclining at the table or the one ministering? Is it not the one reclining at the table? But I am in YOUR midst as the one ministering."**

YHWH: God Almighty. Creator. Father.

YHWH is sovereign over all the earth. (Psalms 83:18) **That people may know that you, whose name is YHWH, You alone are the Most High over all the earth.**

YHWH is the head of Jesus. (1 Corinthians 11:3) **But I want YOU to know that the head of every man is the Christ; in turn the head of a woman is the man; in turn the head of the Christ is God.**

Jesus: Leader of God's Kingdom and head of the congregation of true Christians.

Jesus is son of YHWH. (Matthew 3:17) **"Look! Also, there was a voice from the heavens that said: "This is my Son, the beloved, whom I have approved."**

Jesus is head of Congregation. (Colossians 1:18) …**and he is the head of the body, the congregation. He is the beginning, the firstborn from the dead, that he might become the one who is first in all things.**

YHWH gave Jesus all authority. (Matthew 19:18) **And Jesus approached and spoke to them, saying: "All authority has been given me in heaven and on the earth."**

Jesus has all things (except YHWH) in subjection under him. (1 Corinthians 15:27-28) **For [God] "subjected all things under his feet." But when he says that 'all things have been subjected,' it is evident that it is with the exception of the one who subjected all things to him. But when all things will have been subjected to him, then the Son himself will also subject himself to the One who subjected all things to him, that God may be all things to everyone.**

Real Christians

Real Christians live in accordance with biblical principles. (1 John 5:3)-**For this is what the love of God means, that we observe his commandments; and yet his commandments are not burdensome.**

Real Christians keep themselves clean of the world. (James 1:27) **The form of worship_ that is clean and undefiled from the standpoint of our God and Father is this: to look after orphans_ and widows in their tribulation, and to keep oneself without spot from the world.**

Real Christians love YHWH with all their hearts soul strength. (Matthew 22:37) **He said to him: "'You must love YHWH_ your God with your whole heart and with your whole soul and with your whole mind.'**

Real Christians love their neighbors as themselves. (Matthew 22:39) **The second, like it, is this, 'You must love your neighbor as yourself.'**

Real Christians make disciples of all nations. (Matthew 28:19-20) **Go therefore and make disciples_ of people of all the nations, baptizing them in_ the name of the Father and of the Son and of the holy spirit,[20] teaching them to observe all the things I have commanded YOU. And, look! I am with YOU all the days until the conclusion_ of the system of things."**

YHWH's "true religion," as organized and described from the bible, must have YHWH as the head, Jesus as the delegated leader, and people who live their lives in accordance with biblical principles. For example, Popes are not mentioned in the bible and are outside the will of YHWH. Bishops are not mentioned in the bible and are outside the will of YHWH. Female Elders and Overseers are outside the will of YHWH. If your organization has a pope or a cardinal or female elders and clergy then you are outside the will of YHWH.

How "True Religion" works with reference to the World Powers

YHWH's organization, or True Religion, should not be a part of the world. This means it should be politically neutral. It should not be a power broker.

Jesus was not part of this world and said in his famous John 17 prayer that his followers would also not be a part of this world. (John 17: 15-18) **I request you, not to take them out of the world, but to watch over them because of the wicked one. They are no part of the world, just as I am no part of the world. Sanctify them by means of the truth; your word is truth. Just as you sent me forth into the world, I also sent them forth into the world.**

True Christians are not supposed to be fashioned by the system of things. (Romans 12:1) **Consequently I entreat YOU by the compassions of God, brothers, to present YOUR bodies a sacrifice living, holy, acceptable to God, a sacred service with YOUR power of reason.-And quit being fashioned after this system of things, but be transformed by making YOUR mind over, that YOU may prove to yourselves the good and acceptable and perfect will of God.**

The reason true Christians don't want to be fashioned by worldly systems is that the world is lying in the power of Satan. (1 John 5:19) **We know we originate with God, but the whole world is lying in the [power of the] wicked one.**

Friendship with the world is enmity with God. (James 4:4) **"Adulteresses, do YOU not know that the friendship with the world is enmity with God? Whoever, therefore, wants to be a friend of the world constitutes himself an enemy of God.**

If your religion is a power broker in the world then it is not in accordance with biblical principles and is not true religion. The Catholic Church fought hundreds of wars and killed thousands, if not millions of men. The Catholic Church and the Holy Roman Empire make Hitler and Mussolini look like kind hearted idealists. Just think of Lutheran chaplains in Germany praying for god to bless their soldiers as they went off to kill Americans. Or just think of Lutheran chaplains in the USA praying for god to bless their soldiers as they went off to kill Germans. In the last 200 years the only Christian denomination which has never taken up arms against their brothers are Jehovah's Witnesses. Should make you think. Every other denomination presumes to be fighting on God's side and takes up weapons against other Christian brothers who also wrongly assume they are on God's side. Who decides which side has God's blessing?

True Religion is Built on the Rock of Jesus

YHWH's church would be built on the truth that Jesus is God's son. (Matthew 16: 16-18) **In answer Simon Peter said: "You are the Christ, the Son of the living God." In response Jesus said to him: "Happy you are, Simon son of Jonah, because flesh and blood did not reveal [it] to you, but my Father who is in the heavens did. Also, I say to you, You are Peter, and on this rock-mass. I will build my congregation, and the gates of Hades will not overpower it."**

Many faker Christian organizations claim that the interpretation of Matthew 16:16-18 is that the church would be built upon Peter, and they therefore make up a genealogy of all popes dating back to Peter the disciple. This is wrong.

The rock mass that YHWH's congregation will be built upon is Jesus and knowledge that Jesus is God's son. Furthermore, Jesus is described as a "rock" or a "stone" or a "corner stone" or a "chief corner stone" many times throughout the bible.

Jesus is the chief cornerstone that the builders of the apostate church rejected. (Luke 20:17-18) **But he looked upon them and said: "What, then, does this that is written mean, 'The stone which the builders rejected, this has become the chief cornerstone'? Everyone falling upon that stone will be shattered. As for anyone upon whom it falls, it will pulverize him."**

Jesus was the stone of stumbling. (1 Peter 1:7-8) **It is to YOU, therefore, that he is precious, because YOU are believers; but to those not believing, "the identical**

stone that the builders rejected has become [the] head of [the] corner," and "a stone of stumbling and a rock-mass of offense." These are stumbling because they are disobedient to the word. To this very end they were also appointed.

If you build something, build it on a rock mass. (Matthew 7: 24-25) **Therefore everyone that hears these sayings of mine and does them will be likened to a discreet man, who built his house upon the rock-mass. And the rain poured down and the floods came and the winds blew and lashed against that house, but it did not cave in, for it had been founded upon the rock-mass.**

A little stone will destroy the world's empires. (Daniel 2: 34-35) **You kept on looking until a stone was cut out not by hands, and it struck the image on its feet of iron and of molded clay and crushed them. At that time the iron, the molded clay, the copper, the silver and the gold were, all together, crushed and became like the chaff from the summer threshing floor, and the wind carried them away so that no trace at all was found of them. And as for the stone that struck the image, it became a large mountain and filled the whole earth.**

True Religion's Financial Philosophy

Jesus reminds us that the standard for Christian ministry is "free". (Matthew 10: 8) **YOU received free, give free.**

So if your so called denomination charges for books, charges for magazines, charges for bibles, and charges for conferences, then they are not a representation of the organization Jesus wanted.

Furthermore, if your ministers or priests make as much money as lawyers, politicians, and chief financial officers then they are outside the will of YHWH and do not reflect the way Jesus wanted his church to be organized.

How much money did Jesus make a year? What was his retirement plan? Did he live in the house next to the cathedral and drive a Cadillac? Jesus was a man of little means. In fact, almost all of YHWH's servants were poor. You can't worship YHWH and money. (Matthew 6: 24-25) **No one can slave for two masters; for either he will hate the one and love the other, or he will stick to the one and despise the other. YOU cannot slave for God and for Riches.**

Did you know that a retired priest can earn more money than a practicing doctor or lawyer? Who cares if you believe in the YHWH or not, stay a priest long enough and you can retire to absolute luxury.

If your religion takes up offerings they are outside the will of YHWH. YHWH's organization should be run based off of voluntary, discreet, not mandatory, donations. Did you know that in some places there are church taxes which are automatically deducted from your salary? For example, in Germany, depending upon the state you live in, 8-9% of your income is automatically deducted from your salary as "Kirchensteuer," what means "church tax."

In 2012, the Catholic Church received 5.2 million euros and the Protestant Church received 4.6 million euros only from German Church Taxes. Isn't this Nauseating? These churches disregard the commandments of YHWH so they can follow the traditions of men. Electronic fund transfers to the Vatican bank is not in the bible.

True religion should give away truth for free. If you believe that what you write has the power of life and death then you should give it away for free. Does your religion give away bibles and study materials or does it charge for them? If it charges money, then it is outside the will of YHWH.

True Religion's Dressing and Grooming

Although the inner person is so much more important than the outer person, the way you dress says something about you. Let's do some common sense analysis of what the bible says and point out a few easily identifiable bad examples out there: Catholic leadership, evangelical Protestants, and the Jews.

We don't know for sure if Jesus was rich or poor. But the bible tells us he owned a seamless tunic (John 19:23). A seamless tunic took about six months of hard work to make. So Jesus had the equivalent of a thousand dollar handmade suit. What this means to us is that Jesus did not wear funny clothes. So if you wear a funny looking hat like the pope, you are not doing what Jesus did. Neither did Jesus go to the other extreme and dress too casually. So if you are the faker protestant church minister who wears jeans and a t-shirt then you are not doing what Jesus did.

Jesus was dressed in accordance with his culture and customs, but he was dressed nicely and cleanly and respectably. Jesus wanted to reflect the dignity and cleanliness of his father. So don't dresses like a penguin or a crow, as do all the fakers in the Catholic Church? And don't dress like a punk teenager as do the fakers in the protestant church. Dress in something clean and nice and respectable in accordance with the best of your cultural customs. How do leaders in your denomination dress?

Funny hats are not biblical. Paul never wrote a message to the early church leaders saying "in order for everyone to know that you are a super Christian, you must wear a funny hat." But he did write the opposite in 1 Corinthians 11:4: **Every man that prays or prophesies having something on his head shames his head**.

Furthermore, YHWH instructs us that men <u>should not</u> cover our heads at all. (1 Corinthians 11: 7) **For a man ought not to have his head covered, as he is God's image and glory; but the woman is man's glory.**

If you wear a Yamaka then you are outside the will of YHWH. If you wear a silly hat as part of your ridiculous priest outfit then you are outside the will of YHWH. Read the bible, get rid of your ridiculous clothes, quit your job, and repent. Honoring YHWH should not be a part of a carnival show.

True religion is clothed with the new personality, one which becomes more and more like Jesus's personality. (Colossians 3:10) **and clothe yourselves with the new [personality], which through accurate knowledge is being made new according to the image of the One who created it.**

True religion is clothed with holiness. (Colossians 3:12) **Accordingly, as God's chosen ones, holy and loved, clothe yourselves with the tender affections of compassion, kindness, lowliness of mind, mildness, and long-suffering.**

True religion is clothed with love. (Colossians 3: 14) **But, besides all these things, [clothe yourselves with] love, for it is a perfect bond of union.**

YHWH has a great imagination and His creation is wonderful and colorful. Faker Christians and Catholics and orthodox leaders as well as orthodox Jews evidently hate color, joy and brightness. The bible never says to wear funny clothes and dress like a penguin or crow. The bible never says to wear a funny hat.

YHWH wants his worshipers to be:

- humble (the first will be last)
- be neutral (not mixed up in politics because YHWH's kingdom is not of this world)
- built upon the knowledge of Jesus being YHWH's son (upon this rock I will build my church)
- be generous (you have received freely so give freely)
- dressed cleanly and with dignity (modest),not in funny outfits (cloth yourself with love)
- loving (to YHWH and neighbor)

Chances are your faker church doesn't look like the church described above. Your church's traditions are outside the commandments of YHWH (Matthew 15:3).

23. Baptism must reflect a Pure Heart

Church Hypocrisy / Tradition / Lie: It is OK to get baptized as an infant or as a lukewarm Christian.

Biblical Truth: Learn and become obedient to bible principles. Next, become a disciple of Jesus, following his footsteps closely. Then you can get baptized by someone who has the authority to baptize you.

Being baptized symbolizes becoming a new person. As your old self enters the water you die to your old self and are symbolically washed cleaned. Your new personality emerges, completely focused on honoring YHWH with your life.

Baptism requires three things:

1. a decision by someone mature who accepts the word of God, lives in accordance with biblical principles, and who wants to dedicate his life to honoring YHWH
2. water submersion
3. a male baptizer who accepts the word of God and lives in accordance with biblical principles

Of course there are exceptions. And I would never want to put YHWH in a box. But trust me, you are not the exception.

1: A decision by someone mature who accepts the word of God, lives in accordance with biblical principles, and who wants to dedicate his life to honoring YHWH

Baptism is important. Otherwise Jesus would not have told us to make disciples and to baptize.

(Matthew 28:19) **Go, therefore, and make disciples of people of all the nations, baptizing them in the name of the Father and of the Son and of the Holy Spirit.**

First, you accept the truth and then you are baptized. (Acts 2:41) **So those who gladly accepted his word were baptized, and on that day about 3,000 people were added.**

Baby baptism means nothing. You baby didn't even understand what was going on, let alone make a lifelong decision to serve YWHW. Teach your child to be a disciple of Jesus and when he / she is old enough to fully comprehend what this requires and means, they can get baptized to symbolize their commitment.

Baby baptism isn't biblical. There isn't one example of a baby being baptized in the bible. It is impossible for a baby to understand the word of YHWH, accept the word of YHWH, make a decision to live according to biblical principles, and then to dedicate himself and undergo baptism.

All baptisms in the bible involve mature people aware of the decision they are making. Baptisms are only for those wise enough to fully understand that they are making a lifelong commitment to live for YHWH. This can only be done by truly zealous and wise adolescent children or adults.

Jesus was God's perfect son, and yet he was baptized when he was 30. You are not better than Jesus. Your children are not better than Jesus. Your infant's baptism means nothing in the eyes of YWHW. Only when baptism comes from your child's heart, when he or she is truly committed to loving and serving YHWH, does YHWH accept the baptism.

2: Water Submersion

Baptism signifies being born again. (John 3:3) **In response Jesus said to him: "Most truly I say to you, unless anyone is born again,_ he cannot see the Kingdom of God."** This isn't a literal birth but a symbolic birth. Being totally submerged and wet and messy is a more accurate way to symbolically become new or be born again.

Baptism symbolizes the death of our old selves and being made alive to our new selves. (Romans 6: 3-5) **Or do you not know that all of us who were baptized into Christ Jesus were baptized into his death? So we were buried with him through our baptism into his death, in order that just as Christ was raised up from the dead through the glory of the Father, so we also should walk in a newness of life. If we have become united with him in the likeness of his death, we will certainly also be united with him in the likeness of his resurrection.**

Baptisms requires coming out of the water. (Mark 1:9-10) **In the course of those days, Jesus came from Nazareth of Galilee and was baptized in the Jordan by John. And immediately on coming up out of the water, he saw the heavens being parted and, like a dove, the spirit coming down upon him. And a voice came out of the heavens: "You are my Son, the beloved; I have approved you."**

Although the most important aspect of your baptism is your heart, the physical messiness of being submerged and wet and messy and "coming up out of the water" (Mark 1:10) makes being made new more symbolic, more real, and more like what Jesus did.

Again, I don't want to put YHWH in a box but having a porn-addicted fake protestant minister splash a few drops on your forehead doesn't cut it. You should do what Jesus did and Jesus was dunked and came out of the water.

3: Baptism is done by a male baptizer who accepts the word of God and lives in accordance with biblical principles

Since the leaders of the true religion, as defined in the bible, are men, baptism must be conducted by a man. The baptizer must be a ministerial servant, elder (older man) or overseer. Baptisms by a woman do not count because no woman has authority over a man to preside or officiate at his baptism.

Baptism must be conducted by a righteous man with authority. This is common sense. Would you want a hypocritical man who molests children, doesn't pay his taxes, and has no respect for the word of God baptize you? Of course not. You want your baptism to be done by someone who lives his life consistent with biblical principles. Not everyone in the bible baptized. John baptized many, to include Jesus (Matthew 3: 1-5 and 16-17). There is no biblical record of Jesus baptizing anyone. But Jesus' disciples baptized many.

Your adult baptism by hypocritical or unqualified representatives of the Christendom means nothing. Being baptized into a denomination that prays to saints, worships statues and or Mary, celebrates pagan holidays, violates clear bible principles, and teaches false doctrine means nothing. Learn what the bible actually teaches. Become a disciple of Jesus. And when you fully comprehend what this requires and means, get baptized (for the first time) to symbolize your new life serving YHWH.

Since we are talking about baptism, an outward sign of an inward disposition of purity and commitment to honoring YHWH, let's talk about two modern day variations of superficial and non-sustentative transformations: (1) being "born again" and (2) "accept Jesus as their Lord and savior." Both can be done without having the slightest idea about what being a disciple actually means.

For years many modern day protestant faker churches preach and teach that being "born again" is the end all be all - "non-plus-ultra." If you are born again then you are in. No exceptions. You are going to heaven for sure. But like everyone else in their denomination, they are not transformed into a more Christ-like person, they are not obedient to the word of God, they love the world, they don't love their neighbor, and they are certainly not disciples of Christ. Jesus did not say make people "born again." He said make "disciples."

A disciple follows Jesus's example. A disciple studies and knows the bible, and lives in obedience with the bible. So unless you study the bible, know the bible, and are obedient to biblical principles, you have not been reborn.

Many faker Christians roam the world trying to get people to "accept Jesus as their savior." They corner you at a shopping center and ask you if you have "accepted Jesus as your Lord and savior." Of course the guys that ask this have no idea what they are talking about. Jesus said make disciples, he did not say badger people until they feel so bad that they cry out and admit that they need help, only for you to abandon them, not explain to them what the bible really teaches, and then run off to your other faker Christian friends to brag about "leading someone to Jesus."

These people are immature and need to grow up. It is not about them or you, it is about YHWH. It is about loving Him with your all, and loving your neighbor as yourself. You don't have the first idea what it takes to be a real Christian, a disciple of Jesus. Study the bible, know the bible, be obedient to biblical principles. Then, once you are sure you get it, teach this to others. Obedience to and love for YHWH takes years to teach, not two minutes at a shopping mall.

Baptism symbolizes your commitment to YHWH. That means you bear YHWH's name and reputation. If you live a clean life, like a true disciple of Jesus, and have love for one another, then you glorify the name of YHWH. But if you are disobedient and unclean and worldly, then you blaspheme the name of YHWH. The 10 commandments listed in Exodus 20 and Deuteronomy 5 warn us to not blaspheme the name of YHWH. This doesn't simply mean don't say His name like a curse word, which many of you do and tolerate. It means don't be called by His name or associated with His name and be a hypocrite, a faker, worldly, without love, or disobedient.

Shame on the millions of faker Christians out there who have been baptized because that think they are worthy of being associated with YHWH and yet who live immoral, dirty, worldly, unloving and disobedient lives. You blaspheme the name of YHWH every day and slap Him in the face with your hypocrisy and disobedience.

24. Blood is Sacred

Church Hypocrisy / Tradition / Lie: It is OK to eat or drink or put someone / something else's blood into our bodies.

Biblical Truth: It is unquestionably forbidden to eat or drink or put someone / something else's blood into our bodies.

Life is sacred. Life is in the blood. Therefore, blood is sacred.

Life is in the blood. (Leviticus 17:14) **For the life of every sort of flesh is its blood, because the life is in it. Consequently, I said to the Israelites: "You must not eat the blood of any sort of flesh because the life of every sort of flesh is its blood. Anyone eating it will be cut off.** Back in the times of the law, blood sacrificed to YHWH is what made a sacrifice valuable.

The blood of the Passover sheep saved the Israelites during the time of Passover. (Exodus 12:13) **And the blood must serve as YOUR sign upon the houses where YOU are; and I must see the blood and pass over YOU, and the plague will not come on YOU as a ruination when I strike at the land of Egypt.**

We no longer practice the sacrificial laws since Jesus was the last accepted sacrifice. But if the law tells us that blood is required to make a sacrifice, then the underlying Biblical principles remind us that blood is sacred.

Jesus' blood poured out as the great Passover lamb saves all who believe in him and exercise faith in him. (Matthew 26:27-28) **Also, he took a cup and, having given thanks, he gave it to them, saying: "Drink out of it, all of YOU; for this means my 'blood of the covenant,' which is to be poured out in behalf of many for forgiveness of sins.**

The bible tells us to abstain from blood. (Acts 15:28-29) **For the holy spirit and we ourselves have favored adding no further burden to YOU, except these necessary things, to keep abstaining from things sacrificed to idols and from blood and from things strangled_ and from fornication._ If YOU carefully keep yourselves from these things, YOU will prosper. Good health to YOU!"**

The above scripture is authoritative. With the help of YHWH's power (spirit) the older men (elders) of the early church say that we must abstain from blood. So what does that mean for you?

True Christians don't drink blood.

True Christians don't eat blood.

True Christians don't accept blood transfusions.

True Christians don't accept vaccinations with blood in it.

There are four fractions in blood: Platelets, Plasma, Red Blood Cells and White Blood Cells. True Christians don't accept or use or eat or drink or inject any part of blood.

The medical community is reinforcing the bible's requirement to not mix blood. Science is proving that blood transfusions aren't that safe. This reinforces biblical truth and prevents patients from having complications from someone else's blood or from blood that doesn't match. Bloodless surgeries are becoming more and more common and successful. Bloodless surgeries collect all the blood which flows from the wound or surgery site, clean it, then and put it back into the patient's body during the surgery. Thus people are able to have a major surgery without accepting someone else's blood.

Many cultures and countries have traditional sausages and dishes including blood. These foods are unbiblical and outside the will of YHWH. Don't eat them again.

Some cultures believe it is macho to drink blood. It is not macho. It is unbiblical and outside the will of YHWH. Don't do it.

Blood is sacred and should not be played with, manipulated, consumed or transfused. Honor YHWH with your blood.

Let us now move on to another blood related topic which many Christian denominations don't understand and about which they teach lies: Jesus' blood (sacrifice).

25. Communion is Symbolic

Church Hypocrisy / Tradition / Lie: During communion, the bread mysteriously turns into the body of Jesus and the wine mysteriously turns into the blood of Jesus.

Biblical Truth: Honor Jesus' ransom sacrifice by living a pure and obedient life, not by falsely presuming your powerless and faker Christian priest has turned a wafer into Jesus' skin and wine into his blood.

During Jesus' final meal he started a tradition which many call Communion or the Eucharist. (Luke 22:19-20) **Also, he took a loaf, gave thanks, broke it, and gave it to them, saying: "This means_ my body which is to be given in YOUR behalf. Keep doing this in remembrance of me." Also, the cup in the same way after they had the evening meal, he saying: "This cup means the new covenant by virtue of my blood, which is to be poured out in YOUR behalf."**

Communion is symbolic. This is not open to interpretation.

Many Christian denominations falsely believe that when you participate in communion the bread mysteriously changes into the body of Christ and the wine mysteriously changes into the blood of Christ. These denominations say that only members of their group can partake of the bread and wine because only they understand the miracle that mysteriously occurs when they "partake of the emblems."

Here is a quote from catholic online which explains that they think the bread becomes Jesus's body and the wine his blood: "Recalling these words of Jesus, the Catholic Church professes that, in the celebration of the Eucharist, bread and wine become the Body and Blood of Jesus Christ through the power of the Holy Spirit and the instrumentality of the priest."[14]

If you actually believe you are drinking Jesus' blood then you are a cannibal and are violating YHWH's will. (Acts 15:28-29) **For the holy spirit and we ourselves have favored adding no further burden to YOU, except these necessary things, to keep abstaining from things sacrificed to idols and from blood and from things strangled_ and from fornication._ If YOU carefully keep yourselves from these things, YOU will prosper. Good health to YOU!"**

If what Catholics believe is true then each time a priest does his magical prayer on the wafer and it becomes the living body of Jesus, the priest performs a miracle. According to catholic tradition and requirements, after leading communion three

---

[14] http://www.catholic.org/clife/jesus/eucharist.php

times, the priest would have done three miracles, making him eligible for sainthood. That means every priest should be a saint. Perhaps when they are dead, we can make a medal of them to wear around our necks and pray to them?

Sometimes the bible is not definitive about if a scripture is literal or symbolic. However, when a scripture is presumed to be literal, and by being literal, it violates biblical principles, then this cannot be so because the bible does not contradict itself. Therefore, the communion scriptures must be symbolic.

Since a literal interpretation of communion would mean that we are eating human flesh (cannibalism) and drinking blood (which is also forbidden) then we can know, definitively, that communion cannot be literal.

We are supposed to think of and remember Jesus' broken body (like bread broken in half) and his poured our blood. We are not supposed to do a miraculous prayer to turn a wafer into Jesus' skin so we can become cannibals.

Please know that eating the actual body and drinking the actual blood of Jesus is impossible, weird, super creepy, and a violation of biblical laws and principles.

Communion is symbolic. Think of Jesus' life and sacrifice when you have bread and drink wine. But better yet, the best way to honor Jesus' sacrifice is to live a life consistent with the living word of God.

26. The Bible is the Living Word of God

Church Hypocrisy / Tradition / Lie: The bible is full of wisdom. But it may or may not be relevant for today and may or may not or be inspired by God.

Biblical Truth: Treasure the scriptures, study the scriptures, meditate on the scriptures, and live your life in accordance with the inspired and powerful words of the scriptures.

The bible is where a true Christian gets his or her authority. The bible is either inspired or not. If it is inspired, then you better obey it. If you don't think it is inspired, then you better change your mind soon, before you disqualify yourself from the love of God and everlasting life.

The Bible is not to be interpreted or played with. It is to be obeyed.

The cannon of the bible is not a perfect story because it involves imperfect men and Satan, the deceiver, trying his best to sabotage YHWH's sovereignty. But what we now have is enough to know YHWH and to live in accordance with His principles.

There are good translations of the bible and there are terrible, watered-down translations of the bible. But even in the worse translation of the bible you can find every single biblical principle you need to make YHWH proud of you. Even in a terrible translation you can see that a true Christian should not eat blood, should not watch an R Rated movie, should not fight in a war in support of a secular political nation, should not pray to dead people or Mary, and should not worship images or statues or crosses.

I recommend you use a bible which has Yahweh or YHWH written in it about 7000 times.

Any translator who shows respect to the name of YHWH will also show respect to the words of YHWH.

My wife and I now use online bible reference web-sites which allow us to read the bible in its original language from the oldest scrolls known to exist. We do not fully speak Hebrew, Aramaic, or Greek, but because of these web sites and programs we can study the bible word for word. I can't recommend this enough. These sites are wonderful.[15] The bible was meant to be read, not translated. Sadly the church doesn't teach Hebrew or Greek because it cares more about being relevant and contemporary.

---

[15] www.scripture4all.org

But so much is lost in translation and reading YHWH's word straight from the source is wonderful.

We are so blessed in modern days to have the bible so easily available. But this has not always been the case.

For hundreds of years, the bible was hidden from the people and kept only for the priests to use and interpret. This is how the Catholic Church was able to cheat the people by selling "indulgences" to forgive sin. This was how the Catholic Church was able to claim a lie about the Pope being infallible. If there is any doubt about papal infallibility then check out the endless list of papal mistakes, scandals, and excommunications.

The Catholic Church has locked away other inspired writings. The Catholic Church has tried to hide the name of YHWH. The Catholic Church has even added non-inspired books to what they call the canon of bible literature.

Despite Satan's efforts to hide the word of God, it is available now more than ever. Thanks to a German named Luther, the bible was translated into a common language which has now become standard. Thanks to another German named Gutenberg, the printing press was able to more quickly make bibles for more people to read. Thanks to archeologist who continue to find manuscripts, we know that the Old Testament translations we use now are 99% the same as the scrolls which Jesus himself would have read.

When the oldest copy of the Bible was discovered in Egypt (called the Sinai Codex) the Vatican then displayed their almost complete version (called the Vatican Codex), which is a few years older. Both copies are wonderful.

But how sad is it that the Vatican did not admit to even having their original manuscript until the Sinai Codex was found and announced publicly. If the Vatican actually cared about knowing, teaching, sharing, and doing the will of YHWH, they would have long ago announced the presence of that codex. And let me remind Vatican leaders of one more thing: YHWH knows all the other inspired and stolen documents you have locked within your walls. May YHWH rebuke you.

Thankfully, the Word of YHWH will not pass away. (Mark 13:31) **Heaven and earth will pass away, but my words will by no means pass away.**

You can't stop the word of YHWH from being accomplished. (Isaiah 55:11) **So my word that goes out of my mouth will be._ It will not return to me without results,**

But it will certainly accomplish whatever is my delight,_ And it will have sure success in what I send it to do.

The word of YHWH will be fulfilled. (Luke 16:17) **Indeed, it is easier for heaven and earth to pass away than for one stroke of a letter of the Law to go unfulfilled.**

The Word of God is inspired. (2 Timothy 3:16-17) **All Scripture is inspired of God and beneficial for teaching, for reproving, for setting things straight,_ for disciplining in righteousness, so that the man of God may be fully competent, completely equipped for every good work.**

The word of God is alive. (Hebrews 4:12) **For the word of God is alive and exerts power and is sharper than any two-edged sword and pierces even to the dividing of soul_ and spirit,_ and of joints from the marrow, and is able to discern thoughts and intentions of the heart.**

Sadly, many faker Christians think they are smarter than YHWH and can interpret the bible. They claim that the bible is wrong and then they say things to tickle the ears of the people at the expense of slapping YHWH in the face.

27. Faker Churches Water Down the Truth

Church Hypocrisy / Tradition / Lie: It is OK to play with the bible since it is full of wisdom and may or may not be relevant for today and may or may not or be inspired by God.

Biblical Truth: Don't be content with watered down spiritual milk from your faker Christian denomination. Seek and study and meditate upon hearty spiritual food.

One of the reasons this book needed to be written is because 99% of the people in Christian churches don't know what the bible actually teaches. They are being led by ministers and priests who don't know what the bible actually teaches, and have become satisfied with drinking spiritual milk (for babies) each week rather than eating a spiritual steak (for the mature believer).

Sadly, reading and knowing the Bible is no longer a requirement when studying Theology. What should you learn from a faker church leader who does not even know the source of wisdom?

If you go to a highly liturgical church it is probable that you have no idea what the bible actually teaches. All high liturgy denominations are lukewarm Christian making machines which spend so much effort in peripheral matters that those in the pews never learn anything new or important from the word of God. How sad it is that a 10 year old catholic boy and his 40 year old catholic father both only know that Noah save two of every animal, Moses parted the red sea, Jesus is God, and Mary is the most powerful person in heaven. Do your own research to find that Noah saved not just two but seven of every clean animal, Moses did not part the Red Sea but parted the "Sea of Reeds" or the "Sea of Papyrus," Jesus is not god but is YHWH's son, and Mary is dead and powerless.

Satan has won in those churches by creating people who have become satisfied with mediocrity and accept rituals rather than the life changing wisdom and understanding available if they would only open their pristine, expensive, leather-bound King James Bible.

The fact that this book discusses about 40 biblical doctrines which your church does not know or does not teach epitomizes the fact that your faker church waters down the truth of the bible or exchanges it for the traditions of man. (Matthew 15:3) **In reply he said to them: "Why is it YOU also overstep the commandment of God because of YOUR tradition?"**

Sadly, most people in faker Christian churches are blind, being led by those who are also blind. (Matthew 15:14) **Let them be. A blind guide is what they are. If, then, a blind man guides a blind man, both will fall into a pit.**"

Beware of faker, evil Christians (wolves) dressed in sheep's clothing. (Matthew 7: 15-20) **"Be on the watch for the false prophets that come to YOU in sheep's covering, but inside they are ravenous wolves. By their fruits YOU will recognize them. Never do people gather grapes from thorns or figs from thistles do they? Likewise every good tree produces fine fruit, but every rotten tree produces worthless fruit; a good tree cannot bear worthless fruit, neither can a rotten tree produce fine fruit. Every tree not producing fine fruit gets cut down and thrown into the fire. Really, then, by their fruits YOU will recognize those [men].**

Beware of faker Christian churches which twist the truth. (Acts 20:29-31) **I know that after my going away oppressive wolves will enter in among YOU and will not treat the flock with tenderness, and from among YOU yourselves men will rise and speak twisted things to draw away the disciples after themselves. "Therefore keep awake".**

Human selfishness will cause men to accumulate teachers who don't tell the truth but tell them what they want to hear. (1 Timothy 4:3-4) **For there will be a period of time when they will not put up with the healthful teaching, but, in accord with their own desires, they will accumulate teachers for themselves to have their ears tickled; and they will turn their ears away from the truth, whereas they will be turned aside to false stories.**

The good news is that YHWH sent Jesus to open the eyes of the blind. (Isaiah 42:6-8) **I, YHWH, have called you in righteousness; I have taken hold of your hand. I will safeguard you and give you as a covenant for the people. And as a light of the nations. For you to open the blind eyes, to bring the prisoner out of the dungeon. And those sitting in darkness out of the prison. I am YHWH. That is my name; I give my glory to no one else, and the ears of the deaf will be unstopped.**

To have eyes that see and ears that hear you need to feed on solid spiritual food. (Hebrews 5:11-14) **We have much to say about him, and it is difficult to explain, because you have become dull in your hearing. For although by now you should be teachers, you again need someone to teach you from the beginning the elementary things of the sacred pronouncements of God, and you have gone back to needing milk, not solid food. For everyone who continues to feed on milk is unacquainted with the word of righteousness, for he is a young child. But solid**

food belongs to mature people, to those who through use have their powers of discernment_ trained to distinguish both right and wrong.

Seeking YHWH must be your 1st priority, not your 2nd or 3rd or your 10th. (Matthew 6:33) **Keep on, then, seeking first the Kingdom and his righteousness, and all these other things will be added to you.**

28. YHWH Loves Women

Church Hypocrisy / Tradition / Lie: Women can and should lead the church and family.

Biblical Truth: YHWH loves women and wants them to be empowered, loved, and led by Godly men. But men, not women, were designed by YHWH to lead the church and family.

YHWH loves women.

The heart of a woman is a special gift from YHWH and its unique and wonderful design is a remarkable image of perfection and love.

A woman becomes attracted to the one she loves. She is not influenced at first by handsomeness or beauty but as a result of her love, she develops an unchangeable attraction for the one she has chosen to love. This purity of love is a gift from YHWH.

Men:

- The heart of a woman is so fragile that you must deliberately work with all your strength and discipline to never misuse or hurt this fragile and loving heart.
- Never, never, never hurt a woman's heart.
- YHWH doesn't like it when you mistreat his daughters.
- Do not date for fun. Dating is a word or concept not found in the bible and results in hurting a woman's precious heart.
- Do not flirt or tease or lead on a woman. This builds false expectations and results in hurting a woman's precious heart.
- Stop having sexual or immoral preferences about women. It is wrong to focus on a certain type of woman rather than on her heart. For example… to only say "I like blonds" or "I like big breast" or "I like short hair." Don't focus on things that fade away with age. Your preference should be for someone who loves YHWH. Imagine the self-esteem complexes you will cause if the woman who gives her heart to you is a brunette, with little breasts and long hair. She will not feel loved or cherished because you were evil and had a preference for body types and colors.
- Your true preference should only be to marry a zealous, like-minded Christian who lives in accordance with biblical principles. Women who love YHWH are beautiful. So finding that type of a woman is a win-win situation.

- Your wife should be your standard for beauty. She is the only one you should ever love and desire and treasure and look at-period. Honor her before you even find her.

All true Christian women are beautiful. They are made in YHWH's image and designed to be a helpmate to us, men.

As a father, I am trying hard to teach my daughter how to grow up in this terrible world. I want her to see what right looks like in the family by being a good leader and provider. I want her to see the love I have for her mother, and for YHWH. I want her to know she is loved and that YHWH loves her. I want her to know that to YHWH, she could never be more beautiful. But too often she is insecure about her looks or figure or hair or glasses and doesn't think she is, in fact, beautiful. We struggle to find a balance between taking care of her appearance and not trying to look like the "stars" of this world. It is a struggle to keep her from thinking like the world.

Men, if you don't love your fragile wives well you will not have the approval of YHWH and He will not listen to your prayers. (1 Peter 3:7) **YOU husbands, continue dwelling in like manner with them according to knowledge, assigning them honor as to a weaker vessel, the feminine one, since YOU are also heirs with them of the undeserved favor of life, in order for YOUR prayers not to be hindered.** This scripture is great because it reminds all of us that YHWH's love is undeserved (grace). And it further reminds men that in order to have their prayers heard then men need to treat their wives well.

Women everywhere must be extra thankful to Jesus whose example and teachings valued women so much. The law never said flat out that a man should only have one wife. Yet the biblical principles at work remind us that marriage is sacred and that love should be pure.

Jesus' words during what many call the "sermon on the mount" definitively tell us that a man should only have one wife and that he must remain absolutely loyal to her. (Matthew 5:27-28) **You heard that it was said: 'You must not commit adultery.' But I say to you that everyone who keeps on looking at a woman so as to have a passion for her has already committed adultery with her in his heart.** The expressions "so as to have passion for her" obviously means not to lust or covet, but it also touches upon the truth that the eyes see, then the heart wants.

Jesus is telling men to stop looking at any woman (on the street, in the car beside you, on TV, on the advertisement, or in a magazine) because it will entice your heart to sin.

Polygamy is officially declared immoral and outside the will of YHWH. Jesus tells you to not even look at woman who is not your wife. This is because you are supposed to honor your wife and keep love pure. If you have a second wife it would be impossible to not look at her. So Jesus is mandating that men are to only have one wife.

Sexual sin and lust will prevent you from entering the Kingdom of God. When Jesus says in Matthew 5: 29 that it would be better to have one eye then have both and be thrown into Gehenna (which we know from chapter 14 means total destruction) it is obvious that YHWH doesn't tolerate sexual sin and lust.

Masturbation is immoral. Don't do it. In my opinion, Jesus' reference to the right hand in Matthew 5:30 is a discreet way of saying don't masturbate. Control your sexual urges, wait until you are married, and make a lot of wonderful love with your equally yoked, obedient, loving, real Christian wife.

Women, aren't you glad that Jesus' seven sentences about lust demand men to be loyal to their wives, outlaw polygamy, forbid masturbation, and demand purity within marriage?

Jesus further valued women by allowing them to be a part of His entourage. For example, consider the women traveling with Him when Jesus went to Jerusalem. (Mark 15:40-41) **There were also women watching from a distance, among them Mary Magdalene as well as Mary the mother of James the Less and of Joses, and Salome, who used to accompany him and minister to him when he was in Galilee, and many other women who had come up together with him to Jerusalem.**

YHWH values the education of women. The design of the temple allowed for women to have a place so that they could listen to the Law. They were required to know the law and have it in their heart so that they could teach it to their children. (Deuteronomy 6:4-7) **Listen, O Israel: YHWH our God is one YHWH. You must love YHWH your God with all your heart and all your soul and all your strength. These words that I am commanding you today must be on your heart, and you must inculcate them in your sons and speak of them when you sit in your house and when you walk on the road and when you lie down and when you get.**

YHWH dignified women over 3500 years ago by allowing them to inherit land just like men. Even in the 21st century, many countries and cultures still treat women like property, no better that a car or a farm animal. Read a Jane Austin book to see that even just a century ago "modern countries" threw women out of their husband's house or father's house when the patriarch died.

How wonderful it is that YHWH dignified women by mandating that women share in the inheritance. (Numbers 27: 6-8) **YHWH then said this to Moses: "The daughters of Ze·lo′phe·had are correct. You should by all means give them the possession as an inheritance among their father's brothers and transfer their father's inheritance to them. And tell the Israelites, 'If a man dies without having a son, you must then cause his inheritance to pass to his daughter.**

Women were so loved that they were the first to see and experience the resurrection: Mark 16:1-6.

Women were designed to be helpmates, run the household, and raise wonderful children. YHWH's design for a woman is to be a worker at home. (Titus 2:3-5) **Likewise let the aged women be reverent in behavior, not slanderous, neither enslaved to a lot of wine, teachers of what is good; that they may recall the young women to their senses to love their husbands, to love their children, to be sound in mind, chaste, workers at home, good, subjecting themselves to their own husbands, so that the word of God may not be spoken of abusively.**

YHWH doesn't want women to be the providers. YHWH requires men to provide. (1 Timothy 5:8) **Certainly if anyone does not provide for those who are his own, and especially for those who are members of his household, he has disowned the faith and is worse than a person without faith.** What this means is that all the dead beat husbands out there who do not work to provide for their families or who make their wives work to provide for the families are worse than unbelievers. YHWH places great importance upon accepting your role in life and the woman's role is not to be the provider.

While every part of the body works together, there can only be one head. The leader of the woman is the man. (1 Corinthians 11:3) **But I want YOU to know that the head of every man is the Christ; in turn the head of a woman is the man; in turn the head of the Christ is God.**

Women need to accept their role in YHWH's family. (Ephesians 5: 21-23) **Be in subjection to one another in fear of Christ. Let wives be in subjection to their husbands as to the Lord, because a husband is head of his wife as the Christ also is head of the congregation, he being a savior of [this] body.**

Being in subjection to a Godly man is wonderful. He loves you, cares for you, and provides for you. Who wouldn't want to work for or be partnered with a real Christian man? What a source of strength and love a real Christian man must be. So don't be afraid of the word subjection. (1 John 4:18) **There is no fear in love, but perfect**

love casts_ fear out, because fear restrains us. Indeed, the one who is fearful has not been made perfect in love.

Women should be under the leadership and responsibility and care of their husbands. (Colossians 3:18) **"YOU wives, be in subjection to [your] husbands, as it is becoming in [the] Lord".**

Women, let's be very honest. Being in subjection to a stupid man is very, very hard. And sadly, most men these days are stupid. No wonder modern and liberated women want to lead and assume the man's role. Don't make a mistake and marry a stupid man or a boy. I know that is almost impossible to find a Man of God out there, but it is 100 times better to be lonely than to be linked together with someone stupid.

The difficulty of living a life with someone stupid is why our loving Father reminds women to only marry a man who lives all his life in accordance with biblical truth. The bible warns us not to be unequally yoked with nonbelievers. (2 Corinthians 6:14) **do not become unevenly yoked with unbelievers. For what fellowship do righteousness and lawlessness have? Or what sharing does light have with darkness?**

In the sad case that you are married to someone stupid or you violated biblical guidance and did not marry someone who lives their life in accordance with biblical principles, you must love them so well that they come into the truth. (Peter 3:1-2) **In like manner, YOU wives, be in subjection to YOUR own husbands, in order that, if any are not obedient to the word, they may be won without a word through the conduct of [their] wives, because of having been eyewitnesses of YOUR chaste conduct together with deep respect.**

Women are not supposed to teach or talk from the pulpit in a Christian congregation. (1 Corinthians 14:33-37) **For God is [a God], not of disorder, but of peace. As in all the congregations of the holy ones, let the women keep silent in the congregations, for it is not permitted for them to speak, but let them be in subjection, even as the Law says. If, then, they want to learn something, let them question their own husbands at home, for it is disgraceful for a woman to speak in a congregation. What? Was it from YOU that the word of God came forth, or was it only as far as YOU that it reached? If anyone thinks he is a prophet or gifted with the spirit, let him acknowledge the things I am writing to YOU, because they are the Lord's commandment.**

This last sentence is essential. A woman not speaking in the congregation is the Lord's commandment, not man's. YHWH is simply saying that men must accept their role as leaders, they must accept their responsibility over women, and they must take the lead.

The bible further explains that women are not to teach in a congregation or exercise authority over men. This means they are not supposed to run a church. (1 Timothy 2:12) **I do not permit a woman to teach, or to exercise authority over a man, but to be in silence.**

Women should not go to seminary and become ordained minister for faker Christian denominations. If your church is led by a woman, then your church is outside the will of YHWH.

However, if a woman is in the truth and leading a life in accordance with biblical principles, then she is required to study and know the bible and to "make disciples of all men" in accordance with the great commission. (Matthew 28:19) **Go, therefore, and make disciples of people of all the nations, baptizing them in the name of the Father and of the Son and of the Holy Spirit.** Doing this means that a woman who honors YHWH can teach and instruct and lead bible studies for other women and couples.

Women should only teach men who don't know the bible with the help of their husbands, or in safe numbers.

Women must wear head coverings if they teach in the presence of men. (1 Corinthians 11: 3-6/10) **But I want YOU to know that the head of every man is the Christ; in turn the head of a woman is the man; in turn the head of the Christ is God. Every man that prays or prophesies having something on his head shames his head; but every woman that prays or prophesies with her head uncovered shames her head, for it is one and the same as if she were a [woman] with a shaved head. For if a woman does not cover herself, let her also be shorn; but if it is disgraceful for a woman to be shorn or shaved, let her be covered / That is why the woman ought to have a sign of authority upon her head because of the angels.**

YHWH wants women to have a gentle and mild spirit. (1 Peter 3:3-4) **Do not let your adornment be external—the braiding of hair and the wearing of gold ornaments or fine clothing— but let it be the secret person of the heart in the incorruptible adornment of the quiet and mild spirit, which is of great value in the eyes of God.**

All true Christian women are beautiful. This truth is regardless of age, size, color, nationality and is because a woman who loves YHWH is radiant. No amount of BOTOX or starvation or elective surgeries or physical exercising can ever compare.

Most men are evil these days. Advertisements and the media exploit this evilness to make women insecure about themselves and to entice them to do dumb things or to wear immodest things in order to find a man, get attention, or gain social acceptance.

YHWH did not make women to be two meters tall with 9% body fat. He made a woman's body strong, but soft, feminine, with extra body fat and wide hips to have children. Stop being fashioned after evil magazines, Hollywood / worldly stars, and the expectations of immoral men which want you to be insecure about yourself, dress like prostitutes, buy their products, and vainly fight to look like someone else.

Quit being like the trashy women of the world! Dress modestly, be feminine and colorful, but be modest.

Quit being like the sad women of this world who think of nothing else besides their appearances.

Exercise and treat the temple of your body with respect, but don't be excessive about physical fitness.

Nowhere in the bible does it say that putting yourself under stress to be skinny is good. Making crazy diets or trying to copy anorexic (unhealthy) fashion models from evil magazines is not encouraged in the bible.

In fact, the bible says many times that fatness is good. Isaiah 55:2 tells us: **Why do YOU people keep paying out money for what is not bread, and why is YOUR toil for what results in no satisfaction? Listen intently to me, and eat what is good, and let YOUR soul find its exquisite delight in fatness itself**.

Please note that being overweight is also not healthy or beautiful.

Please have a balance that honors our creator by taking care of your temple, being healthy and feeling well. This will make more time / room in your life to more happily worship God and not be stressed by counting calories very day!

And please accept your essential role in the family, as designed by YHWH. Seek a Godly man who loves you, cares for you, provides for you, takes the lead, and allows you to flourish.

29. Military Chaplains Dishonor YHWH

Church Hypocrisy / Tradition / Lie: It is OK to serve as a chaplain in the military of your country.

Biblical Truth: Chaplains serve Satan and his delegated representatives in the nations in contrast to the will of YHWH and in violation of biblical principles.

Shame on the thousands of faker Christian military chaplains out there who think they represent the living God YHWH. The very fact that you are a part of such a worldly organization exemplifies that you are not a representative of the living God, YHWH. You are immoral, dirty, worldly, unloving and disobedient. You blaspheme the name of YHWH every day and slap Him in the face with your hypocrisy and disobedience.

Let me reuse some ideas from chapter 7 “True Christians Are Separate from the World” so you can see a simple example of how it is impossible to be a real Christian and work for the military.

A faker Christian wants to make a difference in the world so he joins the military of one of the corrupt governments of this world and serves as a chaplain. He prays for soldiers who go off to war in support of that nation’s objectives. But to maintain his job he never has the courage to say that his government, the war, or his commanders are immoral.

He would likely do his best to be politically correct. This faker chaplain is likely as ambitious and as concerned about advancing in rank as the average atheist infantry officer to whom he volunteered to minister.

This faker chaplain knows stories of the bible like a well-educated child but doesn’t live in accordance with biblical principles. This faker Christian supports his nation at the cost of watering down the truth of the scriptures. This faker Christian feels like he is bold when he says “and I pray this in Jesus’ name” and yet is such a faker that he doesn’t even know or use or try to glorify the name of YHWH.

And if he does know the name of YHWH, he is way too afraid to ever say it in public. That would be a career ender for sure. Do you see how working for a government is impossible if you truly love YHWH and want to live in accordance with His principles?

Now let’s imagine a civil war, one like the US Civil War. Just think about hypocritical Baptist chaplains in New York who prayed for God to bless their soldiers as they went off to kill their literal brothers from Virginia. Just think about hypocritical Baptist chaplains in Virginia who prayed for God to bless their soldiers as they went off to kill their literal brothers from New York.

How about an international example? Just think of Lutheran chaplains in Germany praying for God to bless their soldiers as they went off to kill Americans. Or just think of Lutheran chaplains in the USA praying for God to bless their soldiers as they went off to kill Germans. Who decides which side has God's blessing? Maybe the Pope does?

Military chaplains are all wrong, it doesn't matter what country you are from. And this includes the self-righteous USA. The United States is not a nation blessed by YHWH. The USA is not YWHH's nation. The USA is as immoral and as unclean in the eyes of YHWH as China or Syria.

Shame on your corruption, sex scandals in the white house, blood thirsty military, homosexual marriages, millions of abortions, and money worship. Although the currency of the USA has "in God We Trust" written on it, the God of the USA is money and materialism, not YHWH. That is why you are a sinking ship. The USA has inflated their powerless God (money) above YHWH, charged double interest for it to blood thirsty prostitutes throughout the world, and backed it up not with gold or silver but with worthless promises from corrupt politicians and immoral bank leaders.

If you think you can serve as a chaplain in any military force and represent YHWH then you are simply wrong. The reason we don't want to be fashioned by worldly systems is that the world is lying in the power of satan. (1 John 5:19) **We know we originate with God, but the whole world is lying in the [power of the] wicked one.**

Friendship with the World is Enmity with God. (James 4:4) **Adulteresses, do YOU not know that the friendship with the world is enmity with God? Whoever, therefore, wants to be a friend of the world is constituting himself an enemy of God**

Yes, in years past, YHWH blessed and mandated war. But the last time He approved of and mandated war was about 3000 years ago. And when YHWH approved of these wars, He said so through a prophet who actually heard the words of YHWH, to an anointed King, in a specific geographic location, to fulfill a covenant YHWH made with His people. It has been a very long time since YHWH anointed a king, sent messages through prophets to direct that king into war, and provided supernatural power for victory. YHWH does not favor the USA as they kill Iraqis in search of weapons of mass destruction, which evidently did not exist. Honestly, the love of money is perhaps the ultimate weapon of mass destruction and it keeps blowing up daily in the houses of faker Christians around the world.

The "war hungry USA" doesn't have YHWH's blessing just like ISIS, Al-Qaeda and the Taliban don't have YHWH's blessing. A Muslim is simply following a false god and Mohammed his prophet as he wages war against faker Christians throughout the world. The American government is simply following the impulses of their false God mammon as they intervene all over the world. This is Satan's world and for a real Christian it is easy to see Satan (Muslims) fighting Satan (Americans) in a divided house. Because we know from Matthew 12:25 that **"every kingdom divided against itself comes to ruin, and every city or house divided against itself will not stand,"** we know that this system of things will eventually end and true Christians are anxiously awaiting the Kingdom of God.

Jesus said not to live by the sword. (Matthew 26:52) **Put your sword back in its place," Jesus said to him, "for all who draw the sword will die by the sword.**

Jesus's kingdom is not of this world. (John 18:36) **Jesus said, "My kingdom is not of this world. If it were, my servants would fight to prevent my arrest by the Jewish leaders. But now my kingdom is from another place."**

30. The Kingdom of God is Near

Church Hypocrisy / Tradition / Lie: God runs the world. Many of the world's problems are caused by God. God's Kingdom will be when everyone goes to heaven.

Biblical Truth: God's kingdom is not of this world. This world currently lies in the power of the evil one. God's Kingdom is in heaven and on earth, and is coming, soon. So stay awake.

The only solution to the earth's problems is the Kingdom of YHWH. This is why Jesus prayed for YHWH's kingdom to come. (Matthew 6: 9-10) **"YOU must pray, then, this way: "'Our Father in the heavens, let your name be sanctified. Let your kingdom come. Let your will take place, as in heaven, also upon earth.**

How sad it is that the apostate, faker churches out there do not know or use or sanctify the name of YHWH, yet they pray "let your name be sanctified" every day in church and during mass.

How sad it is that the apostate, faker churches out there do not know what the Kingdom of God really is. If you ask the average faker Christian, they will tell you that the kingdom is when we are all dead and living in heaven with Jesus. But that is not so. Jesus spoke so often about the Kingdom of God. Obviously this was an essential item of the faith to understand. Let's look at the Kingdom of God by using the five W's (What, Where, When, Why, Who)

<u>What is the Kingdom of God?</u>

The Kingdom of God is when YHWH will forever establish an incorruptible and loving monarchy with Jesus as the King of Kings.

The Kingdom of God will be righteous government which will end all corruption and bring peace forever. (Daniel 2:44) **And in the days of those kings the God of heaven will set up a kingdom that will never be brought to ruin. And the kingdom itself will not be passed on to any other people. It will crush and put an end to all these kingdoms, and it itself will stand to times indefinite;**

The Kingdom of God will bring all peoples under Jesus' authority. (Psalm 110:1) **The utterance of YHWH to my Lord is: "Sit at my right hand until I place your enemies as a stool for your feet.**

The Kingdom of God will be ruled by Jesus. (Revelation 11:15) **And the seventh angel blew his trumpet. And loud voices occurred in heaven, saying: "The kingdom of the world did become the kingdom of our Lord and of his Christ, and he will rule as king forever and ever."**

The Kingdom of God will be an indefinitely lasting kingdom. (Daniel 7:27) **And the kingdom and the ruler ship and the grandeur of the kingdoms under all the heavens were given to the people who are the holy ones of the Supreme One. Their kingdom is an indefinitely lasting kingdom, and all the ruler ships will serve and obey even them.**

Jesus called the Kingdom of God paradise. (Luke 23:43) **And he said to him: "Truly I tell you today, You will be with me in Paradise."** Please note that in the original scrolls there is a punctuation mark after the word "today." If there was no punctuation mark then Jesus would be saying that that day (immediately after dying) they would be in paradise. But because there is a pause after today, Jesus is saying something similar to "truly right now, today, I am telling you, that when you are resurrected you will receive paradise."

The Kingdom of God will bring everlasting peace. (Isaiah 65:25) **"The wolf and the lamb themselves will feed as one, and the lion will eat straw just like the bull; and as for the serpent, his food will be dust. They will do no harm nor cause any ruin in all my holy mountain," YHWH has said.**

The Kingdom of God will cause war to cease. (Isaiah 2:4) **And they will have to beat their swords into plowshares and their spears into pruning shears. Nation will not lift up sword against nation; neither will they learn war anymore.**

The Kingdom of God will bring perfect health. (Revelation 21:3-4) **With that I heard a loud voice from the throne say: "Look! The tent of God is with mankind, and he will reside with them, and they will be his peoples. And God himself will be with them. And he will wipe out every tear from their eyes, and death will be no more, neither will mourning nor outcry nor pain be anymore. The former things have passed away."**

The Kingdom of God will bring prosperity. (Isaiah 65:21-24) **And they will certainly build houses and have occupancy; and they will certainly plant vineyards and eat [their] fruitage. They will not build and someone else have occupancy; they will not plant and someone else do the eating. For like the days of a tree will the days of my people be; and the work of their own hands my chosen ones will use to the full. They will not toil for nothing, nor will they bring to birth for disturbance; because they are the offspring made up of the blessed ones of**

YHWH, and their descendants with them. And it will actually occur that before they call out I myself shall answer; while they are yet speaking, I myself shall hear.

Where is the Kingdom of God.

The Kingdom of God is on earth and in heaven. Sadly, most faker Christians think that the Kingdom of God will be when we are all resurrected and live like fat baby angels in heaven. But the truth is that the Kingdom of God will keep 99% percent of people on earth.

The Kingdom of God is on earth and in heaven. (Matthew 6:9-10) **"YOU must pray, then, this way: "Our Father in the heavens let your name be sanctified. Let your kingdom come. Let your will take place, as in heaven, also upon earth.**

YHWH gave earth to men. (Psalm 115:16) **As regards the heavens, to YHWH the heavens belong, But the earth he has given to the sons of men.**

YHWH developed the earth so that people could live on it forever. (Isaiah 45:18) **For this is what YHWH has said, the Creator of the heavens, He the [true] God, the Former of the earth and the Maker of it, He the One who firmly established it, who did not create it simply for nothing, who formed it even to be inhabited: "I am YHWH, and there is no one else".**

The righteous will live on earth forever. (Psalm 37:29) **The righteous themselves will possess the earth, And they will reside forever upon it.**

The meek will inherit the earth. (Psalm 37:11) **But the meek ones themselves will possess the earth, And they will indeed find their exquisite delight in the abundance of peace.**

The meek will not go to heaven but will inherit the earth. (Matthew 5:5) **"Happy are the mild-tempered ones, since they will inherit the earth.**

When is the Kingdom of God

The Kingdom of God has not yet begun since it is not a part of the current world system. (John 18:36) **Jesus answered: "My kingdom is no part of this world. If my kingdom were part of this world, my attendants would have fought that I should not be delivered up to the Jews. But, as it is, my kingdom is not from this source."**

Jesus tells his disciples in Matthew 24 many "signs" or indicators of the imminence of His presence and the beginning of the KOG. We should pay attention to these indicators. (Matthew 24:32-33) **Now learn from the fig tree as an illustration this point: Just as soon as its young branch grows tender and it puts forth leaves, YOU know that summer is near. Likewise also YOU, when YOU see all these things, know that he is near at the doors.**

Yet no one knows the day or hour of when the Kingdom of God will come. (Matthew 24: 36-39) **Concerning that day and hour nobody knows, neither the angels of the heavens nor the Son, but only the Father. For just as the days of Noah were, so the presence of the Son of man will be. For as they were in those days before the flood, eating and drinking, men marrying and women being given in marriage, until the day that Noah entered into the ark; and they took no note until the flood came and swept them all away, so the presence of the Son of man will be.**

Why the Kingdom of God

YHWH will vindicate His sacred name. (Ezekiel 36:23) **"And I shall certainly sanctify my great name, which was being profaned among the nations, which YOU profaned in the midst of them; and the nations will have to know that I am YHWH," is the utterance of the Sovereign Lord YHWH, "when I am sanctified among YOU before their eyes."**

The Kingdom of God will bring rejoicing and glory and praise to YHWH. (Revelation 5:13) **And every creature that is in heaven and on earth and underneath the earth and on the sea, and all the things in them, I heard saying: "To the One sitting on the throne and to the Lamb be the blessing and the honor and the glory and the might forever and ever."**

YHWH will take pleasure in His people. (Ezekiel 20:41) **Because of the restful odor I shall take pleasure in YOU, when I bring YOU forth from the peoples and I actually collect YOU together from the lands to which YOU have been scattered, and I will be sanctified in YOU before the eyes of the nations.**

YHWH will take away the reproach of His people. (Isaiah 25:8) **He will actually swallow up death forever, and the Sovereign Lord YHWH will certainly wipe the tears from all faces. And the reproach of his people he will take away from all the earth, for YHWH himself has spoken [it].**

Who lives in the Kingdom of God?

Those who YHWH remembers and calls will enter the Kingdom of God. (Job 13:15) **You will call, and I myself shall answer you. For the work of your hands you will have a yearning.**

Be warned, faker Christians will not enter the Kingdom of God. (1 Corinthians 6:9-10) **What! Do YOU not know that unrighteous persons will not inherit God's kingdom? Do not be misled. Neither fornicators, nor idolaters, nor adulterers, nor men kept for unnatural purposes, nor men who lie with men, nor thieves, nor greedy persons, nor drunkards, nor revilers, nor extortionist will inherit God's kingdom.**

Only a remnant of people will enter the Kingdom of God. (Romans 9:27) **Moreover, Isaiah cries out concerning Israel: "Although the number of the sons of Israel may be as the sand of the sea, it is the remnant that will be saved."**

Only those exercising faith in Jesus will be saved. (John 3:16) **For God loved the world so much that he gave his only-begotten Son, in order that everyone exercising faith in him might not be destroyed but have everlasting life**

Those who exercise faith in Jesus will enter the Kingdom of God. (John 11:25) **Jesus said to her: I am the resurrection and the life. He that exercises faith in me, even though he dies, will come to life.**

The righteous will enter the Kingdom of God. (Psalm 37:29) **The righteous themselves will possess the earth, And they will reside forever upon it.**

The meek will enter the Kingdom of God. (Psalm 37:11) **But the meek ones themselves will possess the earth, And they will indeed find their exquisite delight in the abundance of peace.**

Those who know and use and call upon the powerful name of YHWH will enter the Kingdom of God. (Acts 2:21) **And everyone who calls on the name of YHWH will be saved.**

Those who call upon the name of YHWH will enter the Kingdom of God. (Romans 10:13) **For "everyone who calls on the name of YHWH will be saved."**

Again be warned, faker Christians will not enter the Kingdom of God. Only those who are obedient and do the will of YHWH will enter the Kingdom of God. (Matthew 7:21- 23) **Not everyone saying to me, 'Lord, Lord,' will enter into the kingdom of the heavens, but the one doing the will of my Father who is in the heavens will. Many will say to me in that day, 'Lord, Lord, did we not prophesy in your name, and expel demons in your name, and perform many powerful**

works in your name?' And yet then I will confess to them: I never knew YOU! Get away from me, YOU workers of lawlessness.

Who Rules in the Kingdom of God

YHWH and Jesus will rule in the Kingdom of God. (Revelation 11:15) **And the seventh angel blew his trumpet. And loud voices occurred in heaven, saying: "The kingdom of the world did become the kingdom of our Lord and of his Christ, and he will rule as king forever and ever."**

Of course YHWH is in charge, but He has delegated all authority to Jesus. (Matthew 28:18) **And Jesus approached and spoke to them, saying: "All authority has been given me in heaven and on the earth.**

Jesus and his family are the seed of Abraham and the seed of David who will rule forever. (Psalm 89:3-4) **"I have concluded a covenant toward my chosen one; I have sworn to David my servant, 'Even to time indefinite I shall firmly establish your seed, And I will build your throne to generation after generation.'" Selah.**

Jesus will rule with the assistance of 144,024 specially selected people who will serve as kings and as priests. Only these 144,024 people will go to heaven. The rest of all people will inherit the earth.

24 elders will be with Jesus as He rules the Kingdom of God from heaven. (Revelation 4:4) **And round about the throne [there are] twenty-four thrones, and upon these thrones [I saw] seated twenty-four elders dressed in white outer garments, and upon their heads golden crowns.**

144,000 righteous men will be with Jesus as He rules the Kingdom of God from heaven. (Revelation 14:1) **And I saw, and, look! the Lamb standing upon the Mount Zion, and with him a hundred and forty-four thousand having his name and the name of his Father written on their foreheads.**

The 144,000 will be kings over the earth. (Revelation 5:10) **and you made them to be a kingdom and priests to our God, and they are to rule as kings over the earth".**

When you are one of the 144,024 who will help rule with and serve Jesus from heaven then you will know it. Trust me, it is not you. So please get the idea of going to heaven out of your mind.

When you die and are resurrected, if you are found righteous, you will live forever on a paradise earth. If you are righteous and live through the imminent great tribulation, then you will live forever on paradise earth. Either way, the essential thing for gaining access to the wonderful Kingdom of God is to be righteous.

31. Time Reflects the Evilness of the World Powers

Church Hypocrisy / Tradition / Lie: It is OK to name days of the week and months after false, powerless gods.

Biblical Truth: YHWH's timing is not our own timing.

Time is the word that men use to describe the power that makes thing change.

YHWH's timing is not our timing. A short discussion about this time difference may make us think and perhaps give us a better understanding of reality.

Time was split in half by Jesus, YHWH's Son. Every date in the world is either Before the Common Era (BCE) or Common Era (CE), Before Christ (BC) or After Christ (AC). Christ split time in half.

Sadly, Satan owns the days of the weeks and months of the year because all the days of the week and months of the year are named after false, powerless gods or planets. Think about the names of the days or months and you will find they are named after planets and constellations and false gods.

YHWH commands us not to even mention the name of a false god. (Exodus 23:13) **"And YOU are to be on your guard respecting all that I have said to YOU; and YOU must not mention the name of other gods. It should not be heard upon your mouth.**

If the early Catholic Church truly had honoring YHWH in mind when they made the Gregorian calendar they would not have allowed the names of false gods to be used for days and months.

There are so many calendar errors which dishonor YHWH. We have already highlighted that Jesus was not born on the 25th of December. We know Jesus did not die for our sins during Easter. Jesus paid a ransom for us all on Passover, which according to the bible and the Jewish calendar is the 14th day of Nissan, not some random Sunday in the spring.

How wonderful it will be when YHWH's kingdom comes and we are no longer a part of Satan's evil system of things which includes mentioning the names of false gods whenever we discuss days and months. (Matthew 6:9-10) **Our Father in the heavens, let your name be sanctified. Let your kingdom come. Let your will take place, as in heaven, also upon earth.**

YHWH's biblical calendar is a super accurate Lunar-Solar system. The days of the week have no names, with the exception of the 7th day which is called the Sabbath. The day begins at sundown, and ends about 24 hours later when the sun sets. In the winter, days had very little light. In the summer, there was a lot of light.

There was no time as in "5:00 in the morning." Time started at first light which is why all the bible times are expressions like "in the 3rd hour" or "during the 6th hour." If sunrise is 0600 then the 3rd hour would be about 0900 and the 6th hour would be around 1200, noon. Because in modern times we so completely worship money and productivity and scheduling too many events into our completely overstressed out lives, YHWH's system seems imprecise. But YHWH's original system works perfectly for those who live simply and prioritize the family and loving and serving YHWH. I don't understand how the catholic church in 1538 could justify throwing away YHWH's calendar in order to adopt their Gregorian calendar with false pagan god names for days and months.

YHWH is timeless. (Psalm 90:4) **For a thousand years are in your eyes but as yesterday when it is past, And as a watch during the night.**

With YHWH a day is like a thousand human years. (2 Peter 3:8) **however, let this one fact not be escaping YOUR notice, beloved ones, that one day is with YHWH as a thousand years and a thousand years as one day.**

Yet, YHWH has also placed the desire to live forever in man's heart. (Ecclesiastes 3:11) **Everything he has made pretty in its time. Even time indefinite he has put in their heart, that mankind may never find out the work that the [true] God has made from the start to the finish.**

Our brain's potential validates that YHWH designed us to live forever. Humans use something like 10 percent of our brain. Imagine how smart we would be if we actually used 100% of our YHWH given abilities. For example, a child growing up in a multi-cultural family, learns three languages before she turns four years old and grows up to become a doctor. This smart person uses 10% of her brain's potential. Down the street is an average American teenager who can only speak English, and not without using profanity every fifth sentence. He plays videogames and watches a lot of TV. This dumb person uses only 5% of his brain. Of course, modern society has accepted mediocrity, but even the smart kid only uses a fraction of her brain. This must hint at a design whereby humans can learn and grow and think for centuries. Imagine if that smart kid has everlasting life and how smart she will be in 500 years.

Remember the illustration of the Math Teacher in chapter 3? YHWH is the math teacher and the bible tells us the rules for doing the long division of life. Satan is the troublemaking student who proudly thinks he has a better way to do long division. YHWH could have smashed Satan but instead he lets Satan prove that his way for doing long division is wrong. Only YWHW's rules for life lead to joy and fulfillment and peace and love.

YHWH could have smashed Satan for his disobedience but He decided to allow Satan to prove himself wrong. And that he has done. Satan has proven in the last six thousand years that man cannot rule himself and that only by living a life obedient to YHWH's commandments will man have peace and health and be free from hunger and death and suffering.

How wonderful it will be to see YHWH's Kingdom come. Yet, according to the bible, it has taken almost six thousand years since the fall of Adam and Eve to prove Satan wrong. But what are six thousand years to YHWH, our eternal and timeless Father? They are like 6 days.

If YHWH's Kingdom would have come yesterday or last year then there would have been no hope for you. But He continues to be patient. Perhaps one of the many reasons He is so patient is so you can pick up this book, read it, have your eyes opened to see church hypocrisies and learn biblical truth, and then return to YHWH with all your heart.

Let us consider the loving patience of YHWH. Our loving father wants no one to perish. (2 Peter 3:9) **YHWH is not slow respecting his promise, as some people consider slowness, but he is patient with YOU because he does not desire any to be destroyed but desires all to attain to repentance.**

YHWH is patient and wants everyone to come into an accurate knowledge of Him. (1 Timothy 2:3-6) **This is fine and acceptable in the sight of our Savior, God, whose will is that all sorts of men should be saved and come to an accurate knowledge of truth. For there is one God, and one mediator between God and men, a man, Christ Jesus, who gave himself a corresponding ransom for all.**

Be warned, however. YHWH's patience is running out. Time is running out. Please turn your hearts back to the Father (Malachi 4: 6) and do it soon.

32. Honor the Sabbath on Saturday

Church Hypocrisy / Tradition / Lie: The "Lord's day" is on Sunday.

Biblical Truth: YHWH's gave us the Sabbath so we would rest. He commanded that we honor the Sabbath on Saturday, and that we honor the Sabbath forever.

The best example of your time not being YHWH's time is the Sabbath. YHWH gave the Sabbath to humans and He gave it to us on day 7. The Jewish calendar uses numbers for its days. But the 7th day is special. It has a name. It is called the Sabbath. The Spanish language still calls it "Sabado" or Sabbath day. But in English, we call it Saturday, sadly named after the pagan false god saturn. The catholic church chose to ignore the Saturday Sabbath and now billions of faker Christians celebrate the "day of rest" on Sunday, a day named after the false sun god. If your time was like YHWH's time then you would celebrate the Sabbath on Saturday, like YHWH designed and like the Jews still celebrate.

YHWH gave us the Sabbath as part of the ten commandments. (Exodus 20:8-9) **Remember the Sabbath day to keep it sacred. You are to labor and do all your work for six days, but the seventh day is a Sabbath to YHWH your God.**

YHWH made the Sabbath for man to rest (Mark 2:27-28) **Then he said to them: "The Sabbath came into existence for the sake of man, and not man for the sake of the Sabbath. So the Son of man is Lord even of the Sabbath."**

Jesus came to fulfil the law, not cancel the law. (Matthew 5:17) **"Do not think I came to destroy the Law or the Prophets. I came, not to destroy, but to fulfill.**

Jesus honored the Sabbath. The gospels are full of examples of Jesus honoring the Sabbath, but not being ridiculous and legalistic about following the Sabbath. Jesus still honored His father, rested, and loved others by doing good for them.

Jesus believed in the Sabbath and presumed the Sabbath would be honored up until the great tribulation and the coming of the kingdom of God. (Matthew 24:19-21) **Woe to the pregnant women and those nursing a baby in those days! Keep praying that your flight may not occur in wintertime nor on the Sabbath day; for then there will be great tribulation such as has not occurred since the world's beginning until now, no, nor will occur again.**

God's people will always honor the Sabbath. (Hebrews 4:9) **So there remains a Sabbath-rest for the people of God.**

YHWH never delegated to faker early church "fathers" the ability to change the Sabbath from Saturday to Sunday. Constantine never had permission to change the Sabbath from Saturday to Sunday. But since Constantine was known to worship the sun god then it makes perfect sense that he changed the Sabbath to Sunday and renamed it "the lord's day."

The bigger question is why do billions falsely ignore the Sabbath and rest on the wrong day. Don't they care about what YHWH wants and has ordered thru the bible.

Or do they simply care more about the traditions of men than they do about the commandments of YHWH? (Matthew 15:3) **In reply he said to them: "Why is it YOU also overstep the commandment of God because of YOUR tradition?"**

Please enjoy a gift from YHWH and observe a Sabbath's rest from Friday sunset until Saturday at sundown. This is what Jesus did, and what YHWH mandated for time everlasting.

33. False Miracles Exemplify the Evilness of Faker Religions

Church Hypocrisy / Tradition / Lie: Your minister or priest has miraculous powers and is full of holy spirit.

Biblical Truth: Satan is trying to mislead the entire world and his sophisticated ways have deceived many.

Holy Spirit is YHWH's power and YHWH's power is able to do anything. However, many are deceived by the works of the devil and think they are witnessing miracles from YHWH.

Let's look at these examples.

- People who pray to the "lord" and the "lord" answers back
- People who speak in tongues at faker evangelical churches
- Faith healings at faker evangelical churches
- Faith healings at "holy" catholic sites
- Crying or bleeding statues
- Exorcisms

<u>People who pray to the "lord" and the "lord" answers back.</u>

I have heard many faker Christians say things like "God told me to do this and that" or "I think God is telling me to do this or that."

In all of biblical history, YHWH almost always only spoke through one prophet at a time. Statistical probability indicates that you are not the prophet for this generation.

The prophets YHWH did choose were refined through suffering into being men of absolute purity and devotion to YHWH. They were not sinful "soccer moms" who have fake breasts, a child's understanding of biblical principles, a criminal's obedience to biblical principles, and who pray that "the Lord Jesus" will make them richer so they can drive a nicer car to and from their gossip woman's group bible study. The prophets YHWH chose were not faker Christian men who are lethargic husbands, pray to Jesus rather than YHWH, who love to use fancy doctrinal terms in the pulpit right before having an affair with the youth director's wife.

YHWH's prophets were amazing men of character who had to endure amazing things in order to publish the word of YHWH. I doubt YHWH is now speaking to faker Christians who love looking at porn, play violent video games, and couldn't quote

10 bible verses if their life depended upon it. Trust me, YHWH did not tell you to buy the Cadillac or do an interpretive dance for your congregation during the Easter Sunday service.

If YHWH speaks to you then there is no doubt about it. It makes me sick to hear people say "I think the lord is telling me to do this or that." Daniel saw an angel and fell to his face in fear. John saw an angel and fell on his face in fear. Moses spoke with YHWH and his (Moses') face would glow. If you actually do hear voices then it is the voice of Satan pretending to be Jesus or YHWH. Please repent, clean up your life and house and car and music and friends, study the bible, and the voices in your head will be replaced with your own sound thoughts which reflect and make decisions based upon biblical principles.

<u>People who speak in tongues at evangelical faker churches</u>

Satan and his demons are very successful when they transforms themselves into false angels and ministers. (2 Corinthians 11:14,15) **And no wonder, for Satan himself keeps transforming himself into an angel of light. It is therefore nothing great if his ministers also keep transforming themselves into ministers of righteousness. But their end shall be according to their works.** This is an essential scripture for understanding the lies that many churches and leaders have been telling for years.

This book is an attempt to open the eyes of the ones whose hearts are rightly disposed to see the truth. The reason so many don't see the truth is that they follow the lies and false teachings of their ministers who are following demons pretending to be angels of light or ministers of righteousness.

If demons can overtake men and their entire personalities, as witnessed dozens of times in the four gospels, then it is easy for them to take over a faker Christian and make them talk nonsense for a few minutes in church to make a huge spectacle of themselves and become undignified.

Satan has bombarded the world with many false religions which tell people what they want to hear. (2 Timothy 4:3-4) **For there will be a period of time when they will not put up with the healthful teaching, but, in accord with their own desires, they will accumulate teachers for themselves to have their ears tickled; and they will turn their ears away from the truth, whereas they will be turned aside to false stories.**

The gifts of Holy Spirit were almost always given to help spread the Good News of the Kingdom of God (Mathew 24:14) in the first century. In modern days, YHWH doesn't need to send his power to entire churches to get them to preach the good news in foreign languages. Bibles are available in hundreds of languages and 99% of the people groups of this world have access to the written word.

Furthermore, if your faker church really was a "spirit filled" church then don't you think that YHWH would first use His power to cure your pastor of his porn addiction before he gave every strong willed woman and disobedient man the ability to speak gibberish to one another, without any benefit to the advancement of the Kingdom of God. I don't want to limit the amazing power and capabilities of YHWH and say that the gifts of holy spirit are no longer available, but I will say that they are more like one in a billion and no one in your church is that one in a billion, let alone everyone in your church.

Faith Healings in the faker evangelical church

All too often the faker evangelical church likes to heal people or have a guest minister swing through town to heal people.

I remember as a child a guest minister visiting town who asked us to raise our hands if we wanted to dedicate our lives more fully to "the lord." Of course I raised my hand. This man then called me up front and laid his hand on my forehead and started praying aggressively and pushing me slowly and slowly backwards. I noticed two other men come from back stage and stand behind me. As this visiting pastor pushed my forehead back and back I felt the other two men move in behind me and trap my ankles so that I would fall. Their intent was for me to trip backwards and then they would drag me off stage to make a big show of Holy Spirit in front of the audience. I simply stepped over their feet, took a few steps backwards, exposed their fraud and walked away. The next time someone asks me if I want to serve YHWH with more dedication, I will just keep that between YHWH and myself.

I know firsthand a man who was healed at a "healing service" from his chronic knee problems. He felt so great and was so excited. Sadly enough, a month later his knees were bad again. Worse yet, he is still disobedient to biblical principles, is a mostly dead beat husband, doesn't provide for his wife, worships money and physical fitness, and has a huge lust problem. I guess that the healing never enticed him to go and sin no more. (John 5:14) **After this Jesus found him in the temple and said to him: "See, you have become well. Do not sin anymore, so that something worse does not happen to you."**

The human body is so much stronger than anyone thinks. Ask any policeman and or soldier and they will tell you about people who have had the strength to run with broken legs or on broken feet. Adrenaline allows people to maximize their strength and minimize their pain. Hallucinogenic drugs such as LSD have given skinny drug addicts the strength to break handcuffs. The power of Satan and demon possession is no less powerful than the human will, human strength, adrenaline, or LSD.

A demon possessed man in the time of Jesus used to break chains. (Mark 5: 2-4) **And immediately after Jesus got out of the boat, a man under the power of an unclean spirit met him from among the tombs. His haunt was among the tombs, and up to that time, absolutely no one was able to bind him securely, even with a chain. He had often been bound with fetters and chains, but he snapped the chains apart and smashed the fetters; and nobody had the strength to subdue him.** If Satan can make a man break chains he can make your knees or shoulder feel better, giving you the impression that you were healed.

You will know a faker church that does satanically enabled faith healings by its fruit. (Matthew 7: 15-17) **"Be on the watch for the false prophets that come to YOU in sheep's covering, but inside they are ravenous wolves. By their fruits YOU will recognize them. Never do people gather grapes from thorns or figs from thistles do they? Likewise every good tree produces fine fruit, but every rotten tree produces worthless fruit.**

If the church and its members have no true understanding of YHWH and the Kingdom of God, are not obedient, and have no fruit in the lives of their members, then they clearly do not have YHWH's blessing, to include the amazing power to theatrically heal people.

True Religion is recognized by its love, not by theatrics. (John 13:35) **By this all will know that YOU are my disciples, if YOU have love among yourselves.**

<u>Faith healings in the Catholic Church</u>

Lourdes, France is home of one of the Catholic Church's most ridiculous money making ventures which exploits kindhearted, but ignorant and naïve people. Check out the web site if you have a few minutes.

Satan evidently healed someone in the water years back and in modern times, all day long you can go to mass or take baths in the waters to heal yourself from whatever ailments you have. Beware of taxes and fees associated with visiting this site. But feel free to buy all kinds of rosaries and powerless catholic paraphernalia at the many gift shops. Shame on those who work at this unholy and evil place and especially those who volunteer in the gift shops. (Mark 11:17) **He was teaching and saying to them: "Is it not written, 'My house will be called a house of prayer for all the nations'? But you have made it a cave of robbers."**

At this den of thieves, they have set up a huge statue to the "Lady of Lourdes." As we studied in chapters 17 and 19, we are commanded to worship YHWH, not a dead and powerless woman. Don't forget to stay at a catholic hotel or visit a local restaurant and eat a "John the Baptist burger" with some "Holy Spirit" sauce.

This place exploits naïve, but perhaps pure-hearted tourists and is almost as sad as modern day Jerusalem.

The worse thing is that despite the Catholic Church leaders knowing this place is a fraud and that any display of power actually comes from Satan, they keep selling tickets and rosaries so you can have a "nice experience" and pray to a dead and powerless Mary rather than to the living god, YHWH.

Shame on the Catholic Church for making money off the power of Satan and for not exposing this fraud to the honest hearted ones you so frequently exploit.

<u>Crying Statues</u>

Crying statues are not from YHWH. They are usually a statue of Mary or the false god Buddah. Would YHWH empower a statue of a false god? Never.

Isn't it suspicious that crying statues have never been documented by professionals on video?

Chapter 17 already discusses the fact that we are commanded to worship YHWH, not statues. Chapter 19 reminds us that Mary is dead, powerless, conscious of nothing, and awaiting the resurrection. Chapter 38 summarizes the evilness of the Catholic Church. Add all this together and it is obvious that crying statues get their "miracle" from Satan.

When Satan tempted Jesus, Satan was powerful enough to make Jesus see the entire world. (Matthew 4: 8-9) **Again the Devil took him along to an unusually high mountain and showed him all the kingdoms of the world and their glory. And he said to him: "All these things I will give you if you fall down and do an act of worship to me".**

If Satan can make Jesus, YHWH's perfect and obedient son, see the entire world at once, Satan can easily make faker Christians see things that don't exist. This may explain some car accidents. But for sure it explain why people think they see catholic statues of Mary bleeding from its eyes.

<u>Exorcisms</u>

Casting out demons exemplifies how much effort Satan and his demons go through to deceive humans and keep them away from the truth. Jesus and his disciples cast out many demons. When they cast out demons, they did so by using the power of YHWH.

However, in modern times, a faker Christian drives out a demon with the sign of a cross and in the name of the trinity. We know from chapter 18 that a cross has no power, dishonors Jesus, and disappoints YHWH. We know from chapter 10 that the trinity is unbiblical. So if a man drives out a demon using a cross and the trinity then we know that he is not driving out the demon using the power of YHWH. If the power does not come from YHWH then it must be a show from Satan. This means that Satan is driving out demons. Satan's house is divided and will not stand.

Satan is desperate because he knows his time is short. (Revelation 12:12) **On this account be glad, you heavens and you who reside in them! Woe for the earth and for the sea, because the Devil has come down to you, having great anger, knowing that he has a short period of time."**

A house divided against itself will not stand. (Matthew 12:25-26) **knowing their thoughts, he said to them: "Every kingdom divided against itself comes to ruin, and every city or house divided against itself will not stand. In the same way, if Satan expels Satan, he has become divided against himself; how, then, will his kingdom stand?**

We know that Satan sometimes pretends to be a minister of righteousness. (2 Corinthians 11:14-15) **And no wonder, for Satan himself keeps transforming himself into an angel of light. It is therefore nothing great if his ministers also keep transforming themselves into ministers of righteousness. But their end shall be according to their works.**

Whether you want to believe it or not, Satan orchestrates a hugely sophisticated game of deception whereby one demon possesses a person, another demon makes a person feel miraculously faith healed, another demon speaks to a person and pretends to be God or Jesus, another demon misleads a man and speaks to him a plan to make a new religion which will pull billions of humans away from true worship, another demon tells a person to start a sect and then to have everyone commit suicide, another demon misleads church members into thinking that a cross and the trinity have power, and another demon leaves (or is exercised) out of a person when confronted by the powerless cross and trinity just to make a good show.

Countless other demons work to make men follow the traditions of men rather than the commandments of YHWH. This game is so sophisticated that you better open your eyes to see it before it is too late.

34. Jesus was a Master Builder on Earth and in Heaven

Church Hypocrisy / Tradition / Lie: Jesus started to exist while on earth.

Biblical Truth: Jesus was and is a master builder. He was YHWH's first creation, who existed from times indefinite before now, and thru him all things were made.

Jesus was a master builder in heaven.

Jesus is called the first born of creation. (Colossians 1:15) **He is the image of the invisible God, the firstborn of all creation.**

Jesus helped YHWH make all things. (Colossians 1:16) **because by means of him all other things were created in the heavens and on the earth, the things visible and the things invisible, whether they are thrones or lordships or governments or authorities. All other things have been created through him and for him.**

Jesus helped create humans and is referred to when YHWH says of man let <u>us</u> make him in <u>our</u> image. (Genesis 1:26) **Then God said: "Let <u>us</u> make man in our image, according to <u>our</u> likeness, and let them have in subjection the fish of the sea and the flying creatures of the heavens and the domestic animals and all the earth and every creeping animal that is moving on the earth."**

Please read Proverbs 8:22-31 because it is Jesus talking about his life before the Earth was created. It is a fantastic scripture, one which most people overlook.

It is fun to ponder the wonderful imagination of our loving Father YHWH and His firstborn Jesus who helped Him create all the wonderful things we enjoy here on Earth. Just think of a juicy piece of corn. The seeds are so delicious and sweet. Now flip the seeds to the inside, make them red, round, and even sweeter and you now have a pomegranate. What unique seeds and what variations. Just think of an eagle soaring, or how a humming bird flaps its wings thousands of times a minute. Both are birds and yet so different. Cocoa and coffee beans are my two favorite vegetables. It is amazing how wonderful and complex the world's design is. Doctors still can't fully understand the human body. NASA can only take pictures of space, let alone build it, define it, regulate it, and name it. Our loving Father and His son truly are master builders.

Even during His time on earth, Jesus was a master builder.

Many know Jesus and his father Joseph to be carpenters. (Matthew 13:55) **Is this not the carpenter's son? Is not his mother called Mary, and his brothers James and Joseph and Simon and Judas?**

Carpenter in this verse is from the original Greek word "Tektonos." This word is better translated as stone worker, master builder, craftsman, builder, and carpenter. Look it up if you are hesitant.

Tekton is the root word for rock as in the large rock masses under the earth's surface called "tectonic plates." So it would not be inaccurate to say Jesus worked to help his dad as a carpenter. But it would be more accurate to say he was a stone mason.

Jesus had to spend a lot of time with his education. He also knew a bit about his impending ministry. So it is logical that Jesus did not plan to inherit the family business and become a master-builder like Joseph. But nonetheless, Jesus was perfect and a wonderful son so there is no doubt that when possible, Jesus would help his father, Joseph, and his brothers with master building.

History reveals to us that during the time of Jesus there was plenty of need for master-builders and stone masons to construct buildings for the both the Romans and Jews.

In order to diminish the popularity and influence of the free masons, the Catholics began to translate "tektonos" into carpenter. Hundreds of years later people can see for themselves that the original scrolls say 'tektonos" or master builder / stone mason but they still can't get past their incorrect Sunday school idea that Jesus was a carpenter.

Jesus' significance and teachings and ransom are not changed if he was a carpenter or a painter or a master builder. But this one small example serves to illustrate the influence that Satan has had in the Catholic Church over the years to hide truth. This book is a small attempt to bring to light other, more essential lies and cover ups from false religions.

35. Characteristics of False Religion

Church Hypocrisy / Tradition / Lie: All churches and denominations basically lead to God.

Biblical Truth: You will know false religion by their bad fruit and should, as soon as possible, flee from false religion. By all means seek the truth before it is too late.

This world is lying in the power of the evil one. (1John5:19) **We know we originate with God, but the whole world is lying in the [power of the] wicked one.** This truth is one which many do not want to accept. Of course YHWH is in charge and sovereign and all capable. But Satan runs the world right now. It only takes a minute to see that human governments have failed man, and that starvation, death, sin, and selfishness abound. Is that a reflection of our holy God of love? No way. The only answer to the problems of this world is God's Kingdom, which will set it all straight again. That is why Jesus said in Matthew 9: 9-10 **YOU must pray, then, this way: "Our Father in the heavens, let your name be sanctified. Let your kingdom come. Let your will take place, as in heaven, also upon earth."**

Nothing short of YHWH's kingdom coming will end the evil effects of Satan upon the current system of things.

Beware of false religions. (Matthew 7:15) **Be on the watch for the false prophets that come to YOU in sheep's covering, but inside they are ravenous wolves.**

A tree is known by its fruit. (Matthew 7:16-20) **By their fruits YOU will recognize them. Never do people gather grapes from thorns or figs from thistles do they? Likewise every good tree produces fine fruit, but every rotten tree produces worthless fruit; a good tree cannot bear worthless fruit, neither can a rotten tree produce fine fruit. Every tree not producing fine fruit gets cut down and thrown into the fire. Really, then, by their fruits YOU will recognize those [men].**

Sects and false religion will become widespread, making the peace, neutrality, cleanliness, integrity, and obedience of true religion manifest. (1 Corinthians 11:19) **For there must also be sects_ among YOU, that the persons approved may also become manifest among YOU.**

Protestant churches which water down the word of God are peddlers of the Word of God. (2 Corinthians 2:17) **for we are not peddlers_ of the word of God as many men are, but as out of sincerity, yes, as sent from God, under God's view, in company with Christ, we are speaking.**

False religions are apostates who have drifted away from the truth into traditions of man. Apostates are "someone whose beliefs have changed and who no longer belongs to a religious or political group."[16]

Apostates are veiled by Satan. (2 Corinthians 4:3-4) **If, now, the good news we declare is in fact veiled, it is veiled among those who are perishing, among whom the god_ of this system of things_ has blinded the minds_ of the unbelievers, that the illumination_ of the glorious good news about the Christ,_ who is the image of God, might not shine through.**

Apostates are mentally in the dark. (Ephesians 4:18) **They are in darkness mentally and alienated from the life that belongs to God, because of the ignorance that is in them, because of the insensitivity of their hearts.**

Woe to those who are teachers and leaders in faker Christian churches and to those who are ordained seminary graduates. You have had within your grasp the truths of the bible but have never been able to fully see them or teach them. You will not inherit the kingdom and are sadly preventing others from going in. (Luke 11:52) **"Woe to you who are versed in the Law, because you took away the key of knowledge. You yourselves did not go in, and you hinder those going in!"**

Churches are full of imposters. (2 Timothy 3:13) **But wicked men and impostors will advance from bad to worse, misleading and being misled.**

YHWH will have a reckoning with false religion. (Jeremiah 25:31) **"A noise will certainly come clear to the farthest part of the earth, for there is a controversy that YHWH has with the nations. He must personally put himself in judgment with all flesh. As regards the wicked ones, he must give them to the sword," is the utterance of YHWH.**

YHWH will make a distinction between true and false religion. (Malachi 3:18) **And YOU people will again certainly see [the distinction] between a righteous one and a wicked one, between one serving God and one who has not served him.**

False religion will become stubble. (Malachi 4:1) **"For, look! The day is coming that is burning like the furnace and all the presumptuous ones and all those doing wickedness must become as stubble. And the day that is coming will certainly devour them," YHWH of armies has said, "so that it will not leave to them either root or bough."**

---

[16] http://www.merriam-webster.com/dictionary/apostate

36. Islam, Buddhism, Hinduism, Mormonism and others are False Religions from Satan

Church Hypocrisy / Tradition / Lie: God has many forms. For example, the god of Islam (allah) is the same as YHWH.

Biblical Truth: YHWH is the only God. There is no other. And you are either for Him or against Him. Period.

YHWH is the only God. There is no other. (Isaiah 45:5) **I am YHWH, and there is no one else. With the exception of me there is no God**.

Jesus came to bring division between those who serve YHWH and those who don't. (Luke 12:51) **Do YOU imagine I came to give peace on the earth? No, indeed, I tell YOU, but rather division.**

You are either for Jesus or against Jesus. (Luke 11:23) **He that is not on my side is against me, and he that does not gather with me scatters.**

You are either for YHWH or against YWHW. YHWH's family consists of the truth, His angels, his Kingdom, His son, and true worshipers. Satan's family consists of everything else.

When you see that everything is either for YHWH or against YHWH it is much easier to live a life which honors YHWH.

Islam: The false prophet Mohamed was deceived by Satan or one of his demons who pretended to be a god. I am sure that the false prophet Mohammed believed the voices in his head and that the false prophet Mohamed accurately wrote down what the voices said. Nonetheless, the voices in his head were not from YHWH but were from Satan or one of his demons pretending to be god. What the false prophet wrote down pulls people away from the truth of YHWH, and has caused war and strife and suppression and sadness ever since. Billions of Muslims have been misled from the truth of YHWH because of the lies that this false prophet wrote down. Satan has succeeded to mislead a huge portion of the earth because of lies that he spoke through his false prophet. Please leave this false religion and seek YHWH, the loving God of Truth.

Hinduism: Hindus believe in a god for everything. This strictly violates the truth that YHWH is the only God. Satan again has succeeded to mislead a huge portion of the earth because of this false religion and their belief in thousands of false gods. Please leave this false religion and seek YHWH, the loving God of Truth.

Buddhism: Worshiping a dead peaceful man and praying to a powerless statue of a fat guy is absolutely against the will of YHWH. Satan again has succeeded to mislead a huge portion of the earth because of this false religion and their belief in that powerless, dead man.

Mormonism: Like Muslims, Mormons have a false prophet, Joseph Smith, who was deceived by Satan or one of his demons. I am sure that the false prophet Joseph Smith believed the voices in his head and I am sure that the false prophet Joseph Smith accurately wrote down what the voices said. Nonetheless, what this false prophet wrote down pulls people away from the truth of YHWH and violates biblical principles. Worse of all is that Mormons believe that there are other god's above YHWH, who created YHWH. Polygamy is outside the will of YHWH. Tolerating a year of sex and drinking and sin which allows men to appreciate the evils of the world is ridiculous and outside the will of YHWH. Thankfully, Mormons are nice and peaceful. But don't be deceived by this niceness. What they do and think and believe violates biblical truth. Satan has succeeded to mislead a portion of the earth because of lies that he spoke through one of his false prophets, Joseph Smith. Please leave this false religion and seek YHWH, the loving God of Truth.

37. Ancient Jews Lost YHWH's Favor

Church Hypocrisy / Tradition / Lie: Jews are God's people so who cares that they missed Jesus's coming. We must politically support the nation of Israel.

Biblical Truth: YHWH has abandoned the Israelites and has offered his hand to the obedient ones of the nations who want to worship him in spirit and in truth.

It is said that the Hebrews are YHWH's people. Jesus, himself, was a Hebrew. True, YHWH made many covenants with the Jews. But sadly, the Hebrews were disobedient and left YHWH. As a consequence of their disobedience, YHWH disciplined them, as a loving Father, in an effort to bring them back into obedience and a right relationship. Yet, the Hebrews left YHWH. Finally, Jesus was sent to model obedience and walking with YHWH, and to be the final blood sacrifice, ending sacrifices for all time. After Jesus's sacrifice, YHWH opened up the promises of the Kingdom of God to those right hearted ones from any nation.

The Jews do not have YHWH's favor any more. If you are a Jew and want to have the favor and love of your Creator, then you must become a true Christian and live a life obedient to biblical principles.

The Hebrews left YHWH. (1 Kings 9:8-9) **And this house itself will become heaps of ruins._ Everyone passing by it will stare in amazement and will certainly whistle and say, 'For what reason did YHWH do like that to this land and this house?' And they will have to say, 'For the reason that they left YHWH their God who had brought their forefathers out from the land of Egypt, and they proceeded to take hold of other gods and bow down to them and serve them. That is why YHWH brought upon them this entire calamity.'**

Jesus said that the Hebrew leaders lost YHWH's favor and that YWHW was now going to turn his favor to the nations. (Mathew 21:43) **This is why I say to YOU, The kingdom of God will be taken from YOU and be given to a nation producing its fruits.**

YHWH has stopped blessing the Hebrews. (Matthew 23:38) **Look! YOUR house is abandoned to YOU.**

YHWH has stopped caring for the Hebrews. (Hebrews 8:7-9) **For if that first covenant had been faultless, no place would have been sought for a second; for he does find fault with the people when he says: "'Look! There are days coming,' says YHWH,_ 'and I will conclude with the house of Israel and with the house of Judah a new covenant; not according to the covenant that I made with their**

forefathers in [the] day of my taking hold of their hand to bring them forth out of the land of Egypt, because they did not continue in my covenant, so that I stopped caring for them,' says YHWH."

YHWH cut off Judah. (2 Kings 23:27) **But YHWH_ said: "Judah, too, I shall remove from my sight, just as I have removed Israel; and I shall certainly reject this city that I have chosen, even Jerusalem, and the house of which I have said, 'My name will continue there.'"**

Sons of Israel (Jews in this scripture) are veiled. (2 Corinthians 3:14-15) **But their mental powers were dulled. For to this present day the same veil remains unlifted at the reading of the old covenant,_ because it is done away with by means of Christ. In fact, down till today whenever Moses is read, a veil lies upon their hearts.**

The Israelites left YHWH and sought after other, false gods. (Isaiah 65:11) **But you are among those forsaking YHWH, Those forgetting my holy mountain, Those setting a table for the god of Good Luck, And Those filling up cups of mixed wine for the god of Destiny.**

There are significant consequences for leaving YHWH. (Jeremiah 2:17) **Have you not brought this on yourself, by abandoning YHWH your God, While he was leading you in the way?**

Jesus correctly said that the Jews followed the traditions of men at the expense of neglecting the commandments of YHWH. This can also be said of all major denominations because hypocrites follow traditions of men, not the bible. (Matthew 15:3) **In reply he said to them: "Why is it YOU also overstep the commandment of God because of YOUR tradition?**

The Jews have sadly lost the favor of YHWH. Their sins brought this upon themselves. YHWH has turned His attention to the gentiles. If only the Hebrews would have paid attention, their peace could have become just like a river, and their righteousness could have been like the waves of the sea. (Isaiah 48:18) **If only you would pay attention to my commandments! Then your peace would become just like a river And your righteousness like the waves of the sea.**

38. Who really leads the Catholic Church?

Church Hypocrisy / Tradition / Lie: It is OK to be Catholic.

Biblical Truth: Get out of the Catholic Church because it violates so many biblical truths and doesn't not honor YHWH.

Based upon the information you read in the above chapters, the Catholic Church…

- Hides the name of God, YHWH (pronounced Yahweh)
- Is not obedient to Biblical principles
- Is misled from the truth by Satan and his demons
- Doesn't discourage unwholesome entertainment
- Doesn't discourage evil friendships
- Promotes wars and is an influential part of the political systems of this world
- Is a den of thieves which seeks to make money off the word of YHWH
- Doesn't understand the role and delegated authorities of Jesus
- Teaches the unbiblical doctrine of the trinity even though the truth is that YHWH is the only, true God, Jesus is His son, and holy spirit is another way to describe YHWH's power
- Teaches a lie about Christmas being Jesus' birthday even though it is a pagan holiday to celebrate the winter solstice
- Teaches a lie about Easter being Jesus' resurrection even though Jesus was killed during Passover (Nissan or Abib the 14th) and not during a pagan holiday to celebrate a false fertility god
- Teaches lies about YHWH causing suffering when in fact suffering is not caused by our loving Father but is caused by Satan, sin, and time / unforeseen circumstance
- Teaches unbiblical lies about death and instantaneously going to heaven
- Teaches unbiblical lies about your soul being immortal and floating up to heaven
- Teaches unbiblical lies about hell-fire and judgment and purgatory
- Encourages unbiblical prayers to and worship of images and crosses
- Violates truth and biblical commandments by using the cross for worship
- Shamefully worships Mary, not YHWH alone
- Shamefully prays to Jesus, Mary, and or saints rather than to YHWH alone
- Violates biblical requirements to be fruitful by mandating celibacy for clergy, monks, and nuns
- Is not organized in accordance with biblical principles and guidelines established by early church leaders

- Worthlessly baptizes babies, kids, and adults who don't understand or live lives in accordance with biblical principles
- Doesn't honor YHWH by teaching that blood is sacred
- Reprehensibly teaches a lie about bread and wine miraculously turning into Jesus' body and blood when celebrating communion
- Doesn't believe that the bible is living and active, follows the traditions of men over the principles of the bible, and changes key words and texts in bible translations
- Waters down the truth of the bible
- Doesn't teach the essential and honored role that YHWH gives to women
- Supports unbiblical wars and political systems via military chaplains
- Doesn't understand or teach the Kingdom of God
- Doesn't use YHWH's calendar but created an evil calendar which uses sacrilegious names for days of the week and months of the year
- Ignores YHWH's commandment for a Saturday Sabbath and created a sacrilegious tradition for a "Lord's day" on Sunday
- Shamelessly uses fraudulent "miracles" and "gifts of the holy spirit" just to keep making money from faithful but naive people
- Doesn't understand Jesus' roll as the master-builder
- Tolerates lies from other false religions and doesn't have the courage to stand for the truth
- Never had YHWH's favor and is obviously recognizable as not the true religion

Leaders of the Catholic Church need to beware, YHWH sees the lies that you are teaching and the other lies you are covering up. (Isaiah 29:15) **Woe to those who go to great lengths to conceal their plans from YHWH. Their deeds are done in a dark place, While they say: "Who sees us? Who knows about us?"**

Shame on you Catholic Church for claiming to represent YHWH yet having led the nations into countless wars.

Shame on you Catholic Church for claiming to represent YHWH yet being a silent partner in countless worldwide businesses. You serve Satan and the god of money.

Shame on you catholic church for claiming to represent YHWH yet selling indulgences to forgive sins and only changing that custom when you got caught by those reading the scriptures themselves.

Shame on you catholic church for claiming to represent YHWH yet hiding so many wonderful documents of truth in your libraries.

Shame on you Catholic Church for claiming to represent YHWH yet employing assassins and murderers. You are worse than the faker religious leaders who killed Jesus.

Shame on you catholic church for claiming to represent YHWH yet the last liar-faker- trash bag Pope Benedict was fired not for being in a scandal but for being caught.

Shame on you catholic church for claiming to represent YHWH yet cutting off the hands or feet of nuns who want to leave your services after being exposed to your hypocrisy.

If you are a Catholic then you are a hypocritical Christian. The Catholic Church violates so many biblical truths that it is impossible to be a member and supporter of the Catholic Church and love the truth.

39. Protestant Churches Dishonor YHWH

Church Hypocrisy / Tradition / Lie: It is OK to go to a Protestant Church.

Biblical Truth: Get out of the protestant church because it violates so many biblical truths and doesn't honor YHWH.

Based upon the information you read in the above chapters, the Catholic Church…

- Hides the name of God, YHWH (pronounced Yahweh)
- Is not obedient to Biblical principles
- Is misled from the truth by Satan and his demons
- Doesn't discourage unwholesome entertainment
- Doesn't discourage evil friendships
- Promotes wars and is an influential part of the political systems of this world
- Is a den of thieves which seeks to make money off the word of YHWH
- Doesn't understand the role and delegated authorities of Jesus
- Teaches the unbiblical doctrine of the trinity even though the truth is that YHWH is the only, true God, Jesus is His son, and holy spirit is another way to describe YHWH's power
- Teaches a lie about Christmas being Jesus' birthday even though it is a pagan holiday to celebrate the winter solstice
- Teaches a lie about Easter being Jesus' resurrection even though Jesus was killed during Passover (Nissan or Abib the 14th) and not during a pagan holiday to celebrate a false fertility god
- Teaches lies about YHWH causing suffering when in fact suffering is not caused by our loving Father but is caused by Satan, sin, and time / unforeseen circumstance
- Teaches unbiblical lies about death and instantaneously going to heaven
- Teaches unbiblical lies about your soul being immortal and floating up to heaven
- Teaches unbiblical lies about hell-fire and judgment
- Encourages unbiblical prayers to and worship of images and crosses
- Violates biblical commandments by using the cross for worship
- Shamefully prays to Jesus rather than to YHWH alone
- Is not organized in accordance with biblical principles and guidelines established by early church leaders
- Worthlessly baptizes babies, kids, and adults who don't understand or live lives in accordance with biblical principles
- Doesn't honor YHWH by teaching that blood is sacred

- Reprehensibly teaches a lie about bread and wine miraculously turning into Jesus' body and blood when celebrating communion
- Doesn't believe that the bible is living and active, follows the traditions of men over the principles of the bible, and changes key words and texts in bible translations
- Waters down the truth of the bible
- Doesn't teach the essential and honored role that YHWH gives to women
- Supports unbiblical wars and political systems via military chaplains
- Doesn't understand or teach the Kingdom of God
- Doesn't use YHWH's calendar but follows an evil calendar which uses sacrilegious names for days of the week and months of the year
- Ignores YHWH's commandment for a Saturday Sabbath and follows a sacrilegious tradition for a "Lord's day" on Sunday
- Shamelessly uses fraudulent "miracles" and "gifts of the holy spirit" just to keep making money from faithful but naive people
- Doesn't understand Jesus' roll as the master-builder
- Tolerates lies from other false religions and doesn't have the courage to stand for the truth
- Never had YHWH's favor and is obviously recognizable as not the true religion
-

If you are a Protestant then you are a faker Christian. The protestant church violates so many biblical truths that it is almost impossible to be a member and supporter of the protestant church and love the truth.

Please leave the protestant church immediately and live a life in accordance with biblical principles. A true Christian doesn't need a denomination but needs to be close to YHWH.

40. Recognize True Christians by Love and Obedience

Church Hypocrisy / Tradition / Lie: If you are mostly obedient to the bible and go to church on Sunday then you are a good Christian and go to heaven.

Biblical Truth: YHWH's followers are always obedient to the bible and are recognized by their love.

What YHWH says is inspired and true. Begin studying the bible so that you can honor Him with your life, decisions, thoughts, efforts, and heart, before it is too late.

True Christians are recognized by their love. (John 13:35) **By this all will know that YOU are my disciples, if YOU have love among yourselves.**

True Christians recognize YHWH's sovereignty. (Psalm 83:18) **That people may know that you, whose name is YHWH, You alone are the Most High over all the earth.**

True Christians are associated with YHWH's Name. (Acts 15:14) **Sym′e·on has related thoroughly how God for the first time turned his attention to the nations to take out of them a people for his name.**

True Christians pray for the Kingdom to come. (Matthew 6:9-10) **YOU must pray, then, this way: "Our Father in the heavens, let your name be sanctified. Let your kingdom come. Let your will take place, as in heaven, also upon earth."**

True Christians accept and prioritize the Word of God. (2 Timothy 3:16-17) **All Scripture is inspired of God and beneficial for teaching, for reproving, for setting things straight, for disciplining in righteousness, that the man of God may be fully competent, completely equipped for every good work.**

True Christians have love amongst themselves. (John 13:34) **I am giving YOU a new commandment, that YOU love one another; just as I have loved YOU, that YOU also love one another.**

True Christians are not of this world. (John 18:35-36) **Pilate answered: "I am not a Jew, am I? Your own nation and the chief priests delivered you up to me. What did you do?" 36 Jesus answered: "My kingdom is no part of this world. If my kingdom were part of this world, my attendants would have fought that I should not be delivered up to the Jews. But, as it is, my kingdom is not from this source."**

True Christians are peaceable. (Isaiah 2:4) **And he will certainly render judgment among the nations and set matters straight respecting many peoples. And they will have to beat their swords into plowshares and their spears into pruning shears. Nation will not lift up sword against nation; neither will they learn war anymore.**

True Christians demonstrate fruit of the spirit. (Galatians 5:22, 23) **On the other hand, the fruitage of the spirit is love, joy, peace, long-suffering, kindness, goodness, faith, mildness, self-control. Against such things there is no law.**

True Christians are witnesses of the love of YHWH. (Isaiah 43:10-12) **"YOU are my witnesses," is the utterance of YHWH, "even my servant whom I have chosen, in order that YOU may know and have faith in me, and that YOU may understand that I am the same One. Before me there was no God formed, and after me there continued to be none. I—I am YHWH, and besides me there is no savior." "I myself have told forth and have saved and have caused [it] to be heard, when there was among YOU no strange [god]. So YOU are my witnesses," is the utterance of YHWH, "and I am God.**

True Christians do to others as they would have done to themselves. Only a few find this narrow path. (Matthew 7:12-14) **All things, therefore, that YOU want men to do to YOU, YOU also must likewise do to them; this, in fact, is what the Law and the Prophets mean. Go in through the narrow gate; because broad and spacious is the road leading off into destruction, and many are the ones going in through it; whereas narrow is the gate and cramped the road leading off into life, and few are the ones finding it.**

True Christians use the name of YHWH as a strong tower. (Proverbs 18:10) **the name of YHWH is a strong tower. Into it the righteous runs and is given protection.**

True Christians are recognized by their joyful eyes. (Psalm 19:8) **The orders from YHWH are upright, causing the heart to rejoice; The commandment of YHWH is clean, making the eyes shine.**

True Christians have peace. (Philippians 4:6-8) **Do not be anxious over anything, but in everything by prayer and supplication along with thanksgiving let YOUR petitions be made known to God; and the peace of God that excels all thought will guard YOUR hearts and YOUR mental powers by means of Christ Jesus. Finally, brothers, whatever things are true, whatever things are of serious concern, whatever things are righteous, whatever things are chaste, whatever**

things are lovable, whatever things are well spoken of, whatever virtue there is and whatever praiseworthy thing there is, continue considering these things.

True Christians find their strength in the joy of YHWH. (Nehemiah 8:10) **And he went on to say to them: "Go, eat the fatty things and drink the sweet things, and send portions to the one for whom nothing has been prepared; for this day is holy to our Lord, and do not feel hurt, for the joy of YHWH is YOUR stronghold."**

True Christians shine. (Matthew 5:16) **Likewise let YOUR light shine before men, that they may see YOUR fine works and give glory to YOUR Father who is in the heavens.**

True Christians are recognized by their pleasant aroma in this world. (2 Corinthians 2:14-16) **But thanks be to God who always leads us in a triumphal procession in company with the Christ and makes the odor of the knowledge of him perceptible through us in every place! For to God we are a sweet odor of Christ among those who are being saved and among those who are perishing; to the latter ones an odor issuing from death to death, to the former ones an odor issuing from life to life. And who is adequately qualified for these things?**

True Christians know and teach the difference between what is clean and unclean. (Ezekiel 44:23) **They should instruct my people about the difference between what is holy and what is common; and they will teach them the difference between what is unclean and what is clean.**

True Christians are not stained by the world or traditions of men. (James 1:27) **The form of worship that is clean and undefiled from the standpoint of our God and Father is this: to look after orphans and widows in their tribulation, and to keep oneself without spot from the world.**

There is a 100% correlation between those who use the name of YHWH and those who live according to biblical principles. The previously listed religions do not use the name you YHWH and they are not obedience to biblical truths or principles.

Please, if only you would stop accepting the hypocrisy and tradition based lies of your church. Do what the bible says. YHWH is real. What He says is inspired and true. Begin studying the bible immediately so that you can honor Him with your life, decisions, thoughts, efforts, and heart, before it is too late.

Conclusion / What Now?

I pray that you already have had your eyes opened to the fact that so many of the beliefs of your church come from the hypocritical traditions of men in clear violation of biblical truth.

Knowing and being obedient to Biblical truth is a matter of life and death, everlasting life and judgment. So please be more concerned with gaining the approval of YHWH than your local minister or priest.

Obedience to Biblical truth is important because the consequences of your mistakes and sins may prevent you from receiving what is good. (Jeremiah 5:25) **Your own errors have prevented these things from coming; Your own sins have deprived you of what is good.**

Biblical Truth is important because you reap what you sow. (Galatians 6:7) **Do not be misled: God is not one to be mocked. For whatever a person is sowing, this he will also reap**

Honor YHWH, not your minister, with everything you do. Your goal should be to hear at the end of your life "Well Done Good and Faithful Servant." (Matthew 25:23) **His master said to him: 'Well done, good and faithful slave! You were faithful..."**

Draw close to YHWH and he will draw close to you. (James 4:8) **Draw close to God, and he will draw close to you.**

Follow Biblical truth, not the hypocrisy and traditions of your church. Matthew 15:3 (NLT) **Jesus replied, "And why do you, by your traditions, violate the direct commandments of God?**

If you are looking for a recommendation as to what to do with your new found biblical knowledge….then I recommend you

1. Don't be a hypocrite. Stop follow man made traditions which violate biblical truth. This is going to hurt a bit but will be worth the effort. It is more important to please YHWH than to please your local minister and friends.

2. Be strong. Self-righteous people are going to be angry at you because you want to stand up for what the bible says and no longer want to blindly follow traditions.

3. Rely on YHWH thru prayer and enjoy the peace that He gives you as a result of being obedient to His rules for life.

4. And most importantly….. let your life be governed by love. Lovingly answer people who ask you why you are different? Love YHWH your God and love your neighbor. (Matthew 22: 37-40) **'You must love YHWH your God with your whole heart and with your whole soul and with your whole mind.' This is the greatest and first commandment. The second, like it, is this: 'You must love your neighbor as yourself.' On these two commandments the whole Law hangs, and the Prophets.**

If you have a challenge, ***apply wisdom*** *from the bible.*
If you have a question, ***apply wisdom*** *from the bible.*
If you need help making a decision, ***apply wisdom*** *from the bible.*

WISDOM
ApplyWisdom.com

Apply Wisdom.com is a modern theological consulting firm and online Christian ministry dedicated to providing biblical, insightful, and pragmatic concepts to make your life better.

Although the bible was written between 2000 and 3500 years ago, it is just as relevant and helpful. The bible is the best place to look for strategies, direction, and solutions for modern-day life.

The Apply Wisdom.com team is composed of bible experts whose wisdom and strategies come from decades of practical life experiences, interpreted through a passion for biblical truth and their desire to love Yahweh and help their neighbor.

Weekly, thought provoking blog articles on relevant themes are free. If you subscribe, you get a free daily devotional. Pay a nominal fee to buy a Book or an Executive Summary. And always feel free to make a donation to support our efforts.

Please enjoy and benefit from Apply Wisdom.com's biblical, insightful, and pragmatic concepts to make your life better.

CPSIA information can be obtained
at www.ICGtesting.com
Printed in the USA
BVOW03s0905181017
497997BV00001B/69/P

9 781946 373007